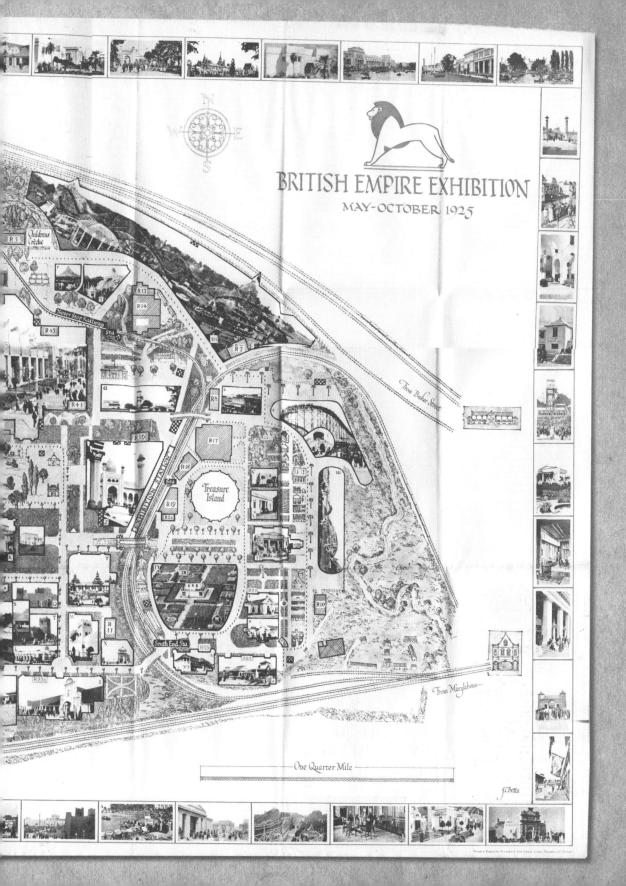

BRITISH EMPIRE EXHIBITION

MAY–OCTOBER 1925

THE GRAND TOUR

Agatha Christie

THE GRAND TOUR

Edited by Mathew Prichard

HarperCollins*Publishers*

Copyright © Christie Archive Trust 2012

Excerpts from *AGATHA CHRISTIE™ An Autobiography*
Copyright © 1977 Agatha Christie Limited. All rights reserved.

Introduction © Mathew Prichard 2012
www.agathachristie.com

Agatha Christie asserts the moral right to
be identified as the author of this work

A catalogue record for this book
is available from the British Library

ISBN: 978 0 00 744768 8

Printed and bound in Spain by
Unigraf

MIX
Paper from
responsible sources
FSC C007454

FSC™ is a non-profit international organisation established to promote
the responsible management of the world's forests. Products carrying the
FSC label are independently certified to assure consumers that they come
from forests that are managed to meet the social, economic and
ecological needs of present and future generations,
and other controlled sources.

Find out more about HarperCollins and the environment at
www.harpercollins.co.uk/green

ACKNOWLEDGMENTS

My grandmother's letters on the Grand Tour were the first, if not the only, part of her archive that my mother, Rosalind, genuinely wanted to share with her public. I would like to take this opportunity of thanking my mother for the dedication, loyalty and intelligence that she always practised where her mother's work was concerned. A big part of Agatha Christie's success and longevity over the years is due to my mother's insistence on quality.

For this volume, I would have been lost without the professionalism of David Brawn and Natasha Hughes at Harper-Collins, designer Rachel Smyth, and the help and encouragement of my wife Lucy.

I would also like to pay tribute to the many fans and friends who have, knowingly and unknowingly, helped me to understand the importance of the legacy my grandmother has left to us all. These include Elaine Wiltshire, John Curran and Joe Keogh, and Robyn Brown and the National Trust at Greenway, but there are many others, most of whom know who they are!

STORIES THAT THRILL

Broothorn Studio.

MRS. AGATHA CHRISTIE

Policewomen are no longer a novelty; the sight of a woman lawyer excites no comment; but a woman writer of detective stories is still somewhat of a pioneer. Mrs. Agatha Christie, at present in Melbourne with her husband, Colonel Christie, a member of the British Empire Mission, which is visiting Australia to make popular the huge exhibition to be held in London in 1924, has written two detective stories. What is more, they have been published by John Lane, and "The Mysterious Affair of Styles" had the unique distinction for a first book of being accepted by "The Times" as a serial for its weekly edition.

"I have never met a detective, nor have I consorted with criminals, as far as I know," was the way Mrs. Christie recently met the query as to whether she went into the "under world" for the copy for her detective stories.

Devonshire and detective stories somehow or other seem incongruous. Yet in Torquay, Devonshire, Mrs. Christie thought out her first story. "It was the result of a bet with my sister," she told. " I had never written a book, and my sister dared me to try to write a detective novel in which the reader could not "spot" the murderer, though having access to the same clues as the detective. "The Mysterious Affair at Styles" is the result of that bet.

Mrs. Christie's early girlhood was spent in trying to decide on a career. She had thoughts of a convent. But she wrote poetry, which was published in the London Bookman and the Poetry Review.

"I don't think I shall ever write poetry again. Detective stories pay so much better," she confessed with a frankness which makes her particularly charming.

In London Colonel and Mrs Christie have a flat. Now they have only one dread—that it will not be big enough to hold the collections they are making in each country they travel through. In South Africa, and now in Australia, they have been attracted by local industries, and from here they go on to New Zealand, Canada, the States, and back to London—and the collection grows.

Talking of the various writing people she knew at home, Mrs Christie had mentioned Marie Corelli. "She lives near where Shakespeare lived," she told, "and she wears white muslin dresses tied up with blue and pink bows. She thinks she is the reincarnation of an Egyptian princess, and objects to anybody else looking like one. When we met I had some Egyptian beads around my hair, so she would hardly speak to me."

Eden Phillpotts lives quite near the Christie home. "He has a great sense of humor, and he grows wonderful pink wallflowers," was the way Mrs Christie summed up this author.

Coming direct from South Africa to Australia, Mrs Christie notices a great difference between the vegetation of the two countries. She is most enthusiastic about the Australian eucalyptus; and the blue of the sky and atmosphere fascinates her. "I have never seen just the same tone of blue anywhere," she insisted.

When she gets back to her London flat and her two-year-old daughter Rosaline, Mrs Agatha Christie may write on what she has observed in her travels. "I think I had better wait until I get a good distance away, and then I'll have time to get the right perspective" was all she would tell about that book.

CONTENTS

—{}–{}—

INTRODUCTION

by Mathew Prichard

By an extraordinary coincidence, it is 20 January 2012 when I sit down to begin writing the introduction to my grandparents' participation in the British Empire Exhibition Mission, known as the Grand Tour, which my grandmother, Agatha Christie, brought so vividly to life in the letters and photographs she sent back to her family. The tour left on 20 January 1922, exactly 90 years ago today.

I called my grandmother *Nima*, presumably a first childish attempt at 'Grandma', and through force of habit I will use this family name in this piece, although of course the events she chronicled took place many years before I was born!

We have to be grateful that these wonderful letters have survived at all. It has been a continual frustration to me, in browsing through family memorabilia, that there are quite a few lovely letters from well-known (and not so well-known) people to Nima, but far fewer of her own letters, which by definition are in the hands of the people to whom she wrote. Fortunately in this case, however, her mother, to whom she wrote the most frequently, did keep the letters; when she sadly died three or four years later, presumably Nima reclaimed them, for they have survived with the rest of the material left by what was, I can promise you, a prolific letter-writing family! As you will see, it was a marvellous bonus to read all the letters for the first time a year or two ago, to see the brief addresses, and to leaf through the old black-and-white photographs, painstakingly pasted into a couple of old photograph albums.

It goes without saying that the world we live in has changed out of all recognition in those 90 years – some would say particularly the places visited on the Empire Tour: South Africa, Australia, New Zealand, Hawaii, and Canada. Not only have the countries changed, but the way we communicate, the way we do business, the way we behave as families – indeed the whole social environment in which people like my grandparents existed has changed so much that it is almost unrecognizable. I think some of the circumstances surrounding the Tour and the people involved would probably have been regarded as fairly eccentric even by their contemporaries, but even so, I think the changes are still very remarkable.

For instance, apart from my grandparents, the chief character concerned, one Major E. A. Belcher, whose last job before initiating this tour was Controller of the Supplies of Potatoes, was obviously a seriously eccentric and difficult man, whose unpredictability and inefficiency sorely tried my grandparents throughout the whole tour. One suspects that his friend and colleagues must have breathed a sigh of relief when they heard that he planned to be out of the country for 10 months! Certainly, however, somebody retained some confidence in him, for the expenses of the trip were considerable – four to seven people's upkeep for 10 months (minus a month's holiday for my grandparents), 'free' passage on ships all the way round the world, 'free' internal travel in each of the countries, not to mention the fees paid to Belcher and my grandfather Archie. At the end of this book I have recorded some evidence about the 1924 British Empire Exhibition. But at the end of the day, who are we to complain – we have gained a charming, perceptive and unconsciously revealing document concerning life shortly after the First World War, written by an author whose gift for storytelling remains second to none from that time to this.

It is worth dwelling for a while on communication. The only methods of communication used by members of the Tour appear to be letters or the occasional necessarily brief telegram. Not only no emails, but no telephones – in other words no immediate form of communication which, for instance, Nima could use to be reassured about the well-being of her two-year-old daughter Rosalind. Letters had to travel by the same means as the tour – by ship! And it appears that in either direction they took weeks or months to arrive, although within its own limitations the system worked very well. Even locally, communications were difficult, which made the keeping of itineraries and timetables challenging, to say the least. Worse, the difficulties of long-distance communication meant Nima and Archie knew before they set out that they would in essence be completely separated from their daughter for 10 months.

From a family point of view Nima and Archie's decision to accompany Belcher on the Grand Tour was brave considering their precarious financial position at the time. I suspect their decision to go arose from Archie's restlessness and dissatisfaction with his current job (a position which might not be kept open for his return); coupled with Nima's passionate desire to see the world, and her suspicion that marriage to a businessman with two weeks' holiday a year would make further opportunities for such adventures non-existent. Sitting at my desk, and reviewing in my mind Nima's life-long love of travel, which took her at various times to the Middle East, North Africa, Sri Lanka, America, the West Indies – sometimes with her family in tow – it is hard to remember that forward vision was not available to her in 1922. She could not see her life spreading out before her, and who are we to blame such a passionate and enthusiastic person for taking what she thought was her one and only chance to see the far end of the world, whatever the financial risks and despite the certainty that she would miss her daughter dreadfully. It is also true to say that 'family support systems', including in Nima's case, a mother, a sister and servants, were much more available and accepted than they are now.

So, Nima and Archie set off and what follows in this book is a completely spontaneous outpouring of wonder at the different people, scenery and events that unfolded before them as they went. Some of what they saw, such as the Victoria Falls, Table Mountain and Sydney Harbour, are still there, though much developed. Much more poignant to me (for I have visited all three cities) were the pictures of Hobart, Wellington, and particularly Cathedral Square in Christchurch, New Zealand. The first two are completely unrecognizable from the buzzing cities you see today. A simple black-and-white picture overwhelms me with a powerful sense of natural elegance and beauty, and, I confess, with a sense of guilt and regret that progress has meant the destruction of something so intrinsically valuable. Christchurch, of course, suffered a devastating earthquake in 2011, but I suspect that if a 1922 resident could see how the city has developed over the intervening decades, he or she would mourn the urban developments almost as poignantly.

One episode which particularly impressed me was Nima's trip to Coochin Coochin Station to visit the Bells, who (as she said) seemed to own most of the cattle in Australia. With their natural vivacity and energy, the Bells provided a stark contrast to the inhibiting nature of Belcher's company; but is it entirely my imagination that the freedom, spontaneity and independence displayed by the Bells on their own patch was something that Nima had never experienced before? I suspect, in good times and in bad, she never forgot it. I remember, in the 1950s, meeting Guilford Bell, Frick's son, who ended up being one of the most innovative and successful architects in Australia, designing some iconic buildings on Sydney Harbour and in Melbourne. I remember him leaving after a weekend with us all and writing in the visitor's book at Greenway, which desperately needed a lick of paint at the time, 'Always paint me white!' I also remember visiting him for dinner in his disarmingly simple (white) house in Melbourne, in which he had decreed that only one picture should be on display in each room. No matter, in the Living Room was one of the most charismatic and glowering landscapes I have ever seen, painted by Russell Drysdale as a gift to Guilford, who had designed a house for him. The Bells, all of them, were an inspiration to Nima. No wonder.

What is one to say about Nima's photography? Ignoring the basic quality of her equipment (she had her camera stolen in South Africa – in my opinion the replacement was better) – it manages to be amazingly evocative. In browsing through the two albums she left us, I couldn't help but admire her assiduousness: the camera must never have left her side. Perhaps this is also a figment of my imagination but I found myself thinking that her photography was like her writing in a different medium – spontaneous, direct, but occasionally with a shaft of brilliant artistic talent. The following is a list of subjects which she photographed that particularly impressed me – all quite different yet each evocative in its own way of the time and place it happened: logging in Canada, surfing in Honolulu, the police in Suva, the youngest cotton picker, trains, Susan in Coochin Coochin, and the 'Bush train'. I will give you no further details – you will enjoy finding them for yourselves.

You would not be surprised to hear that the question I am most often asked about Nima is, 'Yes, but what was she really like?' I have spent, over the past month or so, some time reading these letters and looking at these photographs, and asking myself whether, in the light of what they reveal, my standard answers need to be reviewed. My standard answers were that she was a shy, reserved person, who was very reluctant to talk in public, give press interviews, discuss her work or otherwise engage in activity other than writing books. She was never happier than being with her family or close friends; she was a devout person who believed in God (and in evil) and, to me, an inspirational grandmother far more interested in my own likes and dislikes than in promoting or discussing herself. She was, I have always said, the best listener I ever met. I still believe, based on the evidence of the 25 years or so that I knew her well, that all this is true.

But, as I read her account of the Grand Tour, I see glimpses of another Agatha Christie. One with far more confidence in herself publicly than the one I remember. One who sang in public in Coochin Coochin, was very sociable on board ship, and who had the courage to make the decision to go on the tour and leave her daughter for 10 months. A person who, even though it turned out to be the wrong thing to do, took her place directly beside local dignitaries at the lunch table until being told to go back and sit next to her husband. A young woman of 32 who was actually confident in herself, and in her husband, amid constantly changing circumstances and for the most part in the company of total strangers. One suspects, indeed, that Nima and Archie were the glue that held the tour together, particularly in view of Belcher's unpredictable nature. So I find myself in the presence of a younger Agatha, more confident and assertive than the Nima that I remember – and what do I feel? I feel even more proud of her.

Some three to four years after returning from the tour, as all the world seems to know, Nima had to suffer the death of her mother, and separation and divorce from Archie. As a consequence of these traumatic experiences, she famously got lost, or disappeared, eventually to reappear in Harrogate under another name. It is not appropriate to discuss here the details of this experience, except to say that for most of us the juxtaposition of two of the most disturbing events that can happen to anyone would be life-changing. I am sure Nima was no exception and that a very important part of the confident, carefree wife who accompanied Archie in 1922 was lost forever after the events of 1926–27. From then on, despite a very successful second marriage, all her confidence, energy and genius were concentrated on supporting her new husband and, of course, on her work. The days of vivacious Agatha at public gatherings were not to return; but perhaps in the end we were all the benefactors, for in both quantity and quality her work after 1927 was amazing.

From a historical point of view the account of the Grand Tour, both literary and photographic, is a remarkable snapshot of life in the 1920s, nostalgic and curious. For me it is also a glorious vision of a grandmother I never knew, but who I am very glad existed.

I always think that anybody who ventures to write about Agatha Christie should not bypass her work, and Nima would have agreed. I therefore have to tell you that shortly after the British Empire Mission returned home, Nima published *The Man in the Brown Suit*, an adventure story; and unusually for her, she included a direct portrayal of a real acquaintance – an impersonation of Belcher called Sir Eustace Pedler. Until Belcher objected, he was going to be murdered, but Nima gave him a title ('he will like that,' said Archie). As I never reveal the plots of Nima's stories, all I will say beyond that is that Sir Eustace plays a prominent role! Nima very rarely used real individuals as the basis for her characters, indeed I'm not sure this wasn't the only instance; and she didn't really think it worked. Thus, however, were the many varied characters and events of the Grand Tour given fictional representation. Interestingly, there are those who think that Anne Beddingfield has a marked resemblance to the young and adventurous Agatha too…

Finally, I have tried to interfere with the flow and content of the letters as little as possible. We should all remember that the letters were written 90 years ago in a different social era, and inevitably there is also some repetition, as well as occasional inconsistencies in grammar and punctuation. Many of the captions to the photographs are Nima's own from her albums.

MATHEW PRICHARD
20 January 2012

PREFACE

I had written three books, was happily married, and my heart's desire was to live in the country.

Both Archie and Patrick Spence – a friend of ours who also worked at Goldstein's – were getting rather pessimistic about their jobs: the prospects as promised or hinted at did not seem to materialise. They were given certain directorships, but the directorships were always of hazardous companies – sometimes on the brink of bankruptcy. Spence once said, 'I think these people are a lot of ruddy crooks. All quite legal, you know. Still, I don't like it, do you?'

Archie said that he thought that some of it was *not* very reputable. 'I rather wish,' he said thoughtfully, 'I could make a change.' He liked City life and had an aptitude for it, but as time went on he was less and less keen on his employers.

And then something completely unforeseen came up.

Archie had a friend who had been a master at Clifton – a Major Belcher. Major Belcher was a character. He was a man with terrific powers of bluff. He had, according to his own story, bluffed himself into the position of Controller of Potatoes during the war.

How much of Belcher's stories was invented and how much true, we never knew, but anyway he made a good story of this one. He had been a man of forty or fifty odd when the war broke out, and though he was offered a stay-at-home job in the War Office he did not care for it much. Anyway, when dining with a V.I.P. one night, the conversation fell on potatoes, which were really a great problem in the 1914–18 war. As far as I can remember, they vanished quite soon. At the hospital, I know, we never had them. Whether the shortage was entirely due to Belcher's control of them I don't know, but I should not be surprised to hear it.

'This pompous old fool who was talking to me,' said Belcher, 'said the potato position was going to be serious, very serious indeed. I told him that something had to be done about it – too many people messing about. Somebody had got to take the whole thing over – one man to take control. Well, he agreed with me. "But mind you," I said, "he'd have to be paid pretty highly. No good giving a mingy salary to a man and expecting to get one who's any good – you've got to have someone who's the tops. You ought to give him at least—"' and here he mentioned a sum of several thousands of pounds. 'That's very high,' said the V.I.P. 'You've got to get a good man,' said Belcher. 'Mind you, if you offered it to me, I wouldn't take it on myself, at that price.'

That was the operative sentence. A few days later Belcher was begged, on his own valuation, to accept such a sum, and control potatoes.

'What did you know about potatoes?' I asked him.

'I didn't know a thing,' said Belcher. 'But I wasn't going to let on. I mean, you can do anything – you've only got to get a man as second-in-command who knows a bit about it, and read it up a bit, and there you are!' He was a man with a wonderful capacity for impressing people. He had a great belief in his own powers of organisation – and it was sometimes a long time before anyone found out the havoc he was causing. The truth is that there never was a man less able to organise. His idea, like that of many politicians, was first to disrupt the entire industry, or whatever it might be, and having thrown it into chaos, to reassemble it, as Omar Khayyam might have said, 'nearer to the heart's desire'. The trouble was that, when it came to reorganising, Belcher was no good. But people seldom discovered that until too late.

At some period of his career he went to New Zealand, where he so impressed the governors of a school with his plans for reorganisation that they rushed to engage him as headmaster. About a year later he was offered an enormous sum of money to give up the job – not because of any disgraceful conduct, but solely because of the muddle he had introduced, the hatred which he aroused in others, and his own pleasure in what he called 'a forward-looking, up-to-date, progressive administration'. As I say, he was a character. Sometimes you hated him, sometimes you were quite fond of him.

Belcher came to dinner with us one night, being out of the potato job, and explained what he was about to do next. 'You know this Empire Exhibition we're having in eighteen months' time? Well, the thing has got to be properly organised. The Dominions have got to be alerted, to stand on their toes and to co-operate in the whole thing. I'm going on a mission – the British Empire

Mission – going round the world, starting in January.' He went on to detail his schemes. 'What I want,' he said, 'is someone to come with me as financial adviser. What about you, Archie? You've always had a good head on your shoulders. You were Head of the School at Clifton, you've had all this experience in the City. You're just the man I want.'

'I couldn't leave my job,' said Archie.

'Why not? Put it to your boss properly – point out it will widen your experience and all that. He'll keep the job open for you, I expect.'

Archie said he doubted if Mr Goldstein would do anything of the kind.

'Well, think it over, my boy. I'd like to have you. Agatha could come too, of course. She likes travelling, doesn't she?'

'Yes,' I said – a monosyllable of understatement.

'I'll tell you what the itinerary is. We go first to South Africa. You and me, and a secretary, of course. With us would be going the Hyams. I don't know if you know Hyam – he's a potato king from East Anglia. A very sound fellow. He's a great friend of mine. He'd bring his wife and daughter. They'd only go as far as South Africa. Hyam can't afford to come further because he has got too many business deals on here. After that we push on to Australia; and after Australia New Zealand. I'm going to take a bit of time off in New Zealand – I've got a lot of friends out there; I like the country. We'd have, perhaps, a month's holiday. You could go on to Hawaii, if you liked, Honolulu.'

'Honolulu,' I breathed. It sounded like the kind of phantasy you had in dreams.

'Then on to Canada, and so home. It would take about nine to ten months. What about it?'

We realised at last that he really meant it. We went into the thing fairly carefully. Archie's expenses would, of course, all be paid, and outside that he would be offered a fee of £1000. If I accompanied the party practically all my travelling costs would be paid, since I would accompany Archie as his wife, and free transport was being given on ships and on the national railways of the various countries.

We worked furiously over finances. It seemed, on the whole, that it could be done. Archie's £1000 ought to cover my expenses in hotels, and a month's holiday for both of us in Honolulu. It would be a near thing, but we thought it was just possible.

Archie and I had twice gone abroad for a short holiday: once to the south of France, to the Pyrenees, and once to Switzerland. We both loved travelling – I had certainly been given a taste for it by that early experience when I was seven years old. Anyway, I longed to see the world, and it seemed to me highly probable that I never should. We were now committed to the business life, and a business man, as far as I could see, never got more than a fortnight's holiday a year. A fortnight would not take you far. I longed to see China and Japan and India and Hawaii, and a great many other places, but my dream remained, and probably always would remain, wishful thinking.

'It's a risk,' I said. 'A terrible risk.'

'Yes, it's a risk. I realise we shall probably land up back in England without a penny, with a little over a hundred a year between us, and nothing else; that jobs will be hard to get –

probably even harder than now. On the other hand, well – if you don't take a risk you never get anywhere, do you?'

'It's rather up to you,' Archie said. 'What shall we do about Teddy?' Teddy was our name for Rosalind at that time – I think because we had once called her in fun The Tadpole.

'Punkie' – the name we all used for Madge now – would take Teddy. Or mother – they would be delighted. And she's got Nurse. Yes – yes – that part of it is all right. It's the only chance we shall ever have, I said wistfully.

We thought about it, and thought about it.

'Of course – *you* could go,' I said, bracing myself to be unselfish, 'and I stay behind.'

I looked at him. He looked at me.

'I'm not going to leave you behind,' he said. 'I wouldn't enjoy it if I did that. No, either you risk it and come too, or not – but it's up to you, because *you* risk more than I do, really.'

So again we sat and thought, and I adopted Archie's point of view.

'I think you're right,' I said. 'It's our chance. If we don't do it we shall always be mad with ourselves. No, as you say, if you can't take the risk of doing something you want, when the chance comes, life isn't worth living.'

We had never been people who played safe. We had persisted in marrying against all opposition, and now we were determined to see the world and risk what would happen on our return.

Our home arrangements were not difficult. The Addison Mansions flat could be let advantageously, and that would pay Jessie's wages. My mother and my sister were delighted to have

Rosalind and Nurse. The only opposition of any kind came at the last moment, when we learnt that my brother Monty was coming home on leave from Africa. My sister was outraged that I was not going to stay in England for his visit.

'Your only brother, coming back after being wounded in the war, and having been away for *years,* and you choose to go off round the world at that moment. I think it's disgraceful. You ought to put your brother first.'

'Well, *I* don't think so,' I said. 'I ought to put my husband first. He is going on this trip and I'm going with him. Wives *should* go with their husbands.'

'Monty's your only brother, and it's your only chance of seeing him, perhaps for *years* more.'

She quite upset me in the end; but my mother was strongly on my side. 'A wife's duty is to go with her husband,' she said. 'A husband must come first, even before your children – and a brother is further away still. Remember, if you're not with your husband, if you leave him too much, *you'll lose him.* That's specially true of a man like Archie.'

'I'm sure that's not so,' I said indignantly. 'Archie is the most faithful person in the world.'

'You never know with any man,' said my mother, speaking in a true Victorian spirit. 'A wife *ought* to be with her husband – and if she isn't, then he feels he has a *right* to forget her.'

AGATHA CHRISTIE
from *An Autobiography*

ARCTIC
PEARY LAND
GRANT LD
AXEL HEIBERG I.
ELLESMERE ISLAND
Kane Basin
GREENLAND
PRINCE PATRICK I.
MELVILLE I.
BAFFIN BAY
KEENAN LAND
Melville Sd.
Pt. Barrow
WRANGELL I.
Dolphin and Union Strait
VICTORIA ISLAND
BAFFIN ISLAND
DAVIS STRAIT
Denmark Strait
ALASKA
Nome
St. Michael
Bering Str.
Yukon
Mackenzie R.
Dawson
Gr. Bear L.
C. Navarin
KLONDIKE DISTRICT
MT. ST. ELIAS
Gr. Slave L.
Hudson Bay
LABRADOR
C. Farewell
BERING SEA
KODIAK I.
JUNEAU
ALEUTIAN IS.
Sitka
NORTH
ROCKY MTS
Missouri R.
Winnipeg
NEW FOUNDLAND
Victoria
Quebec
OTTAWA
Montreal
Halifax
Portland
Salt Lake City
Kansas City
Chicago
Boston
Denver
St. Louis
New York
Philadelphia
San Francisco
AMERICA
WASHINGTON
AZORES
Charleston
Mississippi R.
San Diego
New Orleans
BERMUDA IS.
MADEIRA
Galveston
Chihuahua
Havana
TROPIC OF CANCER
Gulf of Mexico
WEST INDIES
Honolulu
HAWAIIAN IS.
MEXICO
CUBA
C. VERDE
Guatemala
Caribbean Sea
Caracas
Georgetown
Paramaribo
Cayenne
PACIFIC
Isthmus of Panama
Bogota
Belem (Para)
Parnahyba
EQUATOR
GALAPAGOS IS.
Quito
Amazon R
Guayaquil
ANDES
MARQUESAS IS. (FR.)
SOUTH AMERICA
Recife
Lima
FIJI IS. (BR.)
Tacna
Sucre
Parana R.
RIO DE JANEIRO
NEW CALEDONIA
TROPIC OF CAPRICORN
Caldera
Asuncion
OCEANIA
EASTER I.
Pelotas
Valparaiso
MONTEVIDEO
Auckland
SANTIAGO
MOUNTAINS
BUENOS AIRES
Valdivia
Wellington
Bahia Blanca
NEW ZEALAND
ATLANTIC OCEAN

SETTING OFF

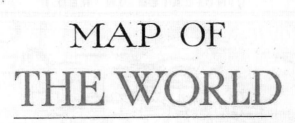

MAP OF

THE WORLD

Showing

BRITISH EMPIRE

and the

EASTERN ASSOCIATED TELEGRAPH COMPANIES' CABLE SYSTEM

"Via Eastern"

Map of
the
World

WATERLOW & SONS LIMITED, LONDON, DUNSTABLE & WATFORD.

Going round the world was one of the most exciting things that ever happened to me. It was so exciting that I could not believe it was true. I kept repeating to myself, 'I am going round the world.' The highlight, of course, was the thought of our holiday in Honolulu. That I should go to a South Sea island was beyond my wildest dream. It is hard for anyone to realise how one felt then, only knowing what happens nowadays. Cruises, and tours abroad, are a matter of course. They are arranged reasonably cheaply, and almost anyone appears to be able to manage one in the end.

When Archie and I had gone to stay in the Pyrenees, we had travelled second-class, sitting up all night. (Third class on foreign railways was considered to be much the same as steerage on a boat. Indeed, even in England, ladies travelling alone would never have travelled third class. Bugs, lice, and drunken men were the least to be expected if you did so, according to Grannie. Even ladies' maids always travelled second.) We had walked from place to place in the Pyrenees and stayed at cheap hotels. We doubted afterwards whether we would be able to afford it the following year.

DOMINION MISSION LEA

The Dominion Mission of the British Empire Exhibition le
picture shows the members of the Mission and their wives, who
left to right they are:—Mr. F. W. Bates (secretary), Mrs. Chri
E. A. Belcher (assistant general manager of the Exhibition, who
and Mr. F. Hiam (agricultural adviser).

ES FOR AFRICA.

The first newspaper cutting from Agatha's photo album. The Times *caption mistakes Miss Hiam for Mrs Christie.*

ndon yesterday for their extended tour. The
companying them, at Waterloo Station. From
Colonel A. Christie (financial adviser), Major
charge of the Mission), Mrs. Hiam, Miss Hiam,

Now there loomed before us a luxury tour indeed. Belcher, naturally, had arranged to do everything in first-class style. Nothing but the best was good enough for the British Empire Exhibition Mission. We were what would be termed nowadays V.I.P.s, one and all.

Mr Bates, Belcher's secretary, was a serious and credulous young man. He was an excellent secretary, but had the appearance of a villain in a melodrama, with black hair, flashing eyes and an altogether sinister aspect.

'Looks the complete thug, doesn't he?' said Belcher. 'You'd say he was going to cut your throat any moment. Actually he is the most respectable fellow you have ever known.'

Before we reached Cape Town we wondered how on earth Bates could stand being Belcher's secretary. He was unceasingly bullied, made to work at any hour of the day or night Belcher felt like it, and developed films, took dictation, wrote and re-wrote the letters that Belcher altered the whole time. I presume he got a good salary – nothing else would have made it worth while, I am sure, especially since he had no particular love of travel. Indeed he was highly nervous in foreign parts – mainly about snakes, which he was convinced we would encounter in large quantities in every country we went to. They would be waiting particularly to attack *him*.

Although we started out in such high spirits, my enjoyment at least was immediately cut short. The weather was atrocious. On board the *Kildonan Castle* everything seemed perfect until the sea took charge. The Bay of Biscay was at its worst. I lay in my cabin groaning with sea-sickness. For four days I was prostrate, unable to keep a thing down. In the end Archie got the ship's doctor to have a look at me. I don't think the doctor had ever taken sea-sickness seriously. He gave me something which 'might quieten things down,' he said, but as it came up as soon as it got inside my stomach it was unable to do me much good. I continued to groan and feel like death, and indeed *look* like death; for a woman in a cabin not far from mine, having caught a few glimpses of me through the open door, asked the stewardess with great interest: 'Is the lady in the cabin opposite dead yet?' I spoke seriously to Archie one evening. 'When we get to Madeira,' I said, 'if I am still alive, I am going to get off this boat.'

'Oh I expect you'll feel better soon.'

'No, I shall never feel better. I must get off this boat. I must get on dry land.'

'You'll still have to get back to England,' he pointed out, 'even if you did get off in Madeira.'

'I needn't,' I said, 'I could stay there. I could do some work there.'

'What work?' asked Archie, disbelievingly.

It was true that in those days employment for women was in short supply. Women were daughters to be supported, or wives to be supported, or widows to exist on what their husbands had left or their relations could provide. They could be companions to old ladies, or they could go as nursery governesses to children. However, I had an answer to that objection. 'I could be a parlour-maid,' I said. 'I would quite *like* to be a parlour-maid.'

Parlour-maids were always needed, especially if they were tall. A tall parlour-maid never had any difficulty in finding a job

– read that delightful book of Margery Sharp's, *Cluny Brown* – and I was quite sure that I was well enough qualified. I knew what wine glasses to put on the table. I could open and shut the front door. I could clean the silver – we always cleaned our own silver photograph frames and bric-à-brac at home – and I could wait at table reasonably well. 'Yes,' I said faintly, 'I could be a parlour-maid.'

'Well, we'll see,' said Archie, 'when we get to Madeira.'

However, by the time we arrived I was so weak that I couldn't even contemplate getting off the bed. In fact I now felt that the only solution was to remain on the boat and die within the next day or two. After the boat had been in Madeira about five or six hours, however, I suddenly felt a good deal better. The next morning out from Madeira dawned bright and sunny, and the sea was calm. I wondered, as one does with sea-sickness, what on earth I had been making such a fuss about. After all, there was nothing the matter with me really, I had just been sea-sick.

There is no gap in the world as complete as that between one who is sea-sick and one who is not. Neither can understand the state of the other. I was never really to get my sea-legs. Everyone always assured me that after you got through the first few days you were all right. It was not true. Whenever it was rough again I felt ill, particularly if the boat pitched – but since on our cruise it was mostly fair weather, I had a happy time.

The R.M.S Kildonan Castle *sailed via Madeira for Capetown, Angola, East London and Natal from Southampton on the 20th January 1922.*

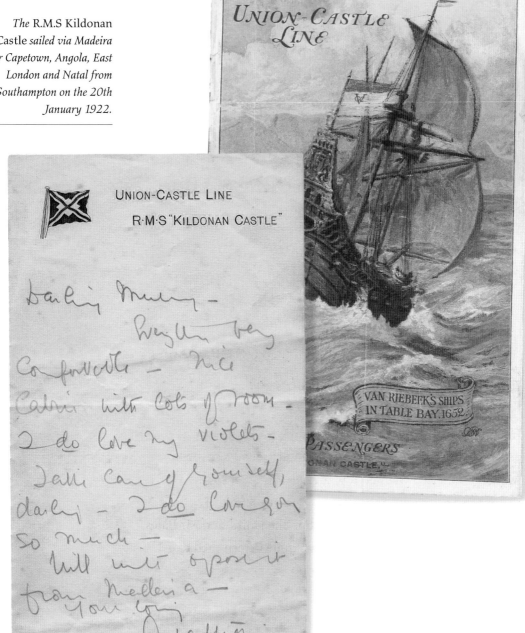

Darling Mummy —

Everything very comfortable — Nice Cabin with lots of room — I do love my violets — Take care of yourself, darling — I do love you so much — Will write oposit from Madeira —

Your loving
Agatha

UNION-CASTLE LINE
R.M.S 'KILDONAN CASTLE'

First day: 20 January 1922

Darling mummy

Everything very comfortable – nice cabin with lots of room.
I do love my violets. Take care of yourself, darling – I do love
you so much.

Will write again from Madeira.

Your loving

Agatha

R.M.S KILDONAN CASTLE

[undated]

Darling Mummy,

I couldn't send you an amusing and cheerful letter from
Madeira because I was laid low, and nearly dead! I was terribly
ill – it was very rough and everyone was ill. Archie, Belcher,
and Hiam were all right, of course but 'the ladies' and Mr Bates
were very sorry for themselves. I was quite determined to get
off at Madeira and come straight home, or take a Villa there
for the winter. The day before we got there, I was very bad. Sick
without ceasing, having tried everything from champagne and
brandy to dry biscuits and pickles, and my arms and legs were

R M S Kildonan Castle

Darling Mummy

I couldn't send you an amusing and cheerful letter from Madeira because I was laid low, and nearly dead! I was terribly ill _ it was very rough and everyone was ill. Archie, Belcher, and Hiam were all right, of course, but " the ladies" and Mr Bates were very sorry for themselves. I was quite determined to get off at Madeira and come straight home, or take a Villa there for the winter. The day before we got there, I was very bad, sick without ceasing, having tried everything from champagne and brandy to dry biscuits and pickles, and my arms and legs were all going pins and ne needly and dead, so Archie fetched the doctor along, and he gave me teaspoonful doses of something or other, chloroform stuff, which stopped the sickness, and nothing to eat for twenty four hours, and then Brand's beef essence. When we got to Madeira, Archie got me up on de deck, and fed me with it, whilst I almost wept because Madeira looked so beautiful. I'd no idea of it. It looked like Kinderscout put bang on the sea, green hills and ravines with houses perched on then like Upper House, or rather like Dartmouth. It was grey weather too, so it must look even more beautiful in sunshine. I couldn't go asho ashore of course, which was rather disappointing.

But since then, I've been quite all right, and am now enjoying m myself hugely, feel perfectly well, have baths and meals, and get up in the morning just as though it was dry land

Your loving

Agatha

all going pins and needly and dead, so Archie fetched the doctor along, and he gave me teaspoonful doses of something or other, chloroform stuff, which stopped the sickness, and nothing to eat for twenty four hours, and then Brand's beef essence. When we got to Madeira, Archie got me up on deck, and fed me with it, whilst I almost wept because Madeira looked so beautiful! I'd no idea of it. It looked like Kinderscout put bang on the sea, green hills and ravines with houses perched on them like Upper House, or rather like Dartmouth. It was grey weather too, so it must look even more beautiful in sunshine. I couldn't go ashore of course, which was rather disappointing.

But since then, I've been quite all right, and am now enjoying myself hugely, feel perfectly well, have baths and meals, and get up in the morning just as though it was dry land.

From henceforth I shall write you a kind of diary, a little every day. I need hardly say that Belcher was at once made chairman of the Sports Committee on board. The boat is not very full. There is rather a nice sailor lad called Ashby going out to join a ship at Cape Town, who went with Mrs Tweedale over the haunted house in Torquay, a delightful woman, Miss Wright, belonging to some college out in South Africa who is most amusing, a Miss Gold who is the thinnest girl I have ever seen and like a Botticelli Madonna, and a particularly fat fellow called Samels with a very nice wife and kiddies. He's a great ostrich person, and the Mission is fixing up a meeting with him out there. We have trained the Chief Engineer, at whose table we sit, to drink 'Success to the Mission' every night, which he does, murmuring. 'But I'm still not sure what kind of a mission it is. They say it's not religious.'

The Hiams are nice, but dull. Won't do anything – enter for quoits or take part in things. Archie and I entered bravely for everything, had our first contest yesterday, when to our utter surprise, we knocked out two Belgians who have infuriated the ship by hanging on to the quoits and practising all day long. It was a most popular victory. Everyone kept coming up to us and saying 'I hear you've knocked out the Dagoes! Splendid.'

Belcher gave us a screaming description of his visit to the King. Whilst airily chatting to Wigram on arrival, a super footman approached and murmured 'which links would you wish

Agatha, and Archie in his tropical suit.

to wear this evening sir?' 'Oh any links, any links,' said Belcher, to which the footman hissed in an agitated whisper: 'I can't find any.' 'And then, of course, I had to take the brass ones out of the shirt I was wearing and hand them to him. Most unfortunate!' The King was charming and most natural, and the Queen had a full description of all the ladies accompanying the Mission, and made a note of my book. Princess Mary was not at all a dump, but very jolly, but Lascelles was a dull dog, who said little, and drank champagne in enormous quantities! They talked a good deal about 'their boy'. The Queen said 'My boy has had thirty five wooden caskets presented to him when he was in Australia, and of course he doesn't know what to do with them. Lovely wood, but hideously made.' The King told a story of Hughes starting out to drive with the Prince through Sydney. 'He started in a topper, but when they got to the suburbs, he hid it under the seat and produced a bowler, and by the time they got to the slums be was wearing a check cap!' He spoke very warmly of Smuts, and

Aboard ship.

said Belcher reminded him of Redmond, and that Ireland would not be in the state it was if Redmond had lived. Two braces of pheasants were presented to Belcher on leaving, and we ate them on board last night, served with great éclat and ceremony!

Very hot now and lots of porpoises leaping, and I've just seen a flying fish! We passed the Grand Peak of Tenerife on Wednesday, and saw the Cape Verde lights last night. No more land now until Cape Town.

Captain Sir Benjamin Chave KBE (far left), Chief Officer Mr D. Nicoll and Chief Engineer Mr A. Munro.

Saturday [February 4]

We had the children's Sports today, and I was asked to give away the prizes, an honour procured for me by Belcher, as against the rival claims of Mrs Blake (wife of the Captain of

the Queen Elizabeth) B. pointing out that I was of equal rank, being the wife of a Colonel in the Army, and had taken some interest in the Sports, Mrs Blake having taken none! She looks very amusing, spends all day talking to a long lean brown Commissioner for Nyasaland. I shall talk to her soon because I like the look of her.

Mr Hiam and Mr Samels had a long and mysterious discussion on pigskin last night, H. declaring there was no such thing, S. saying there was, and that he would show him the

skins, to which H. countered by saying 'Ah, but can you show me a pig being skinned,' and S. climbed down, and said he could not say more before the ladies. I had no idea pigskin was such a delicate subject. It seems to rank with *bech de mer*!

We've had several Bridge fours with Samels. It always takes a least three hours to finish a rubber, because he and Belcher never stop overcalling their hands, and doubling. On the whole Belcher pushes Samels a little further than Samels pushes Belcher! S. has promised me something very choice in ostrich

Mr Mayne.

*Jack and Betty, the Aerial
Sensation perform on the
After Deck.*

feathers if we come to Port Elizabeth. I am now waiting for
someone to ask me if I like diamonds or gold nuggets!

There are some Dutch people, the Fichardts, I believe she
was a daughter of President Stein, and they are violently anti-
English. Belcher spent a whole evening talking to them last
night, and this morning is writing the result in his Diary, and
sending an 'Extract' to the King! We are sending a wedding
present to Princess Mary from South Africa, and he has
promised the Queen an Album of photos of the Mission and its
doings!

There is a Mr Edge on board, a rich elderly bachelor, who
takes thousands of photos all day long. He has made nine
voyages to the Cape and back, never lands – just likes the trip.

The great daily excitement, of course is the 'sweep' on
the day's run. 1/ tickets, and if you draw a number, it is most

Agatha in her 'Chariots and Horses' outfit.

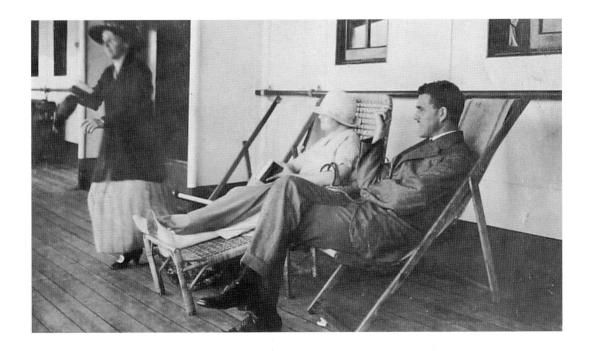

Mrs Blake and Mr Murray.

thrilling. I've drawn a number nearly every day. My one today was a good one, and sold in the Auction for a pound. Not fancying my luck, I've never bought one in so far, but let them go for what they'd fetch – luckily as it proves, but Archie bought his in yesterday for 25/ and got second – £5 15/! Belcher, by common acclamation, is always auctioneer, with Samels (in a terrible green and white striped shirt!) as clown of the piece, and there is a little American called Mayne who does most of the bidding. He is rather nice, dances beautifully, and deals in 'grain elevators' (as much of a mystery to me as 'filled cheese' was to you). We had a fancy dress dance last night, and he was very serious about his costume. 'I have a costume, period 1840, and a costume, period 1830, and a costume 1820!' In

UNION-CASTLE LINE R.M.S. *"KILDONAN CASTLE"*

KILDONAN CASTLE

in the Isle of Arran, is a ruin, a two-storied keep, overlooking the Sound of Pladda and Pladda Island with its lighthouse. It is believed to have been one of a line of watch-towers extending from the mouth of the Clyde to Dumbarton. It was a royal castle until 1405, and is now owned by the Duke of Hamilton.

MENU

DINNER
— ()-() —

Petits Delices, Parisienne

Clear Turtle

Velouté Africaine

Turbot à la Waleska

Ox Tongue Cutlets, Alexandra

Baron of Lamb à la Menthe

Roast Suckling Pig, Anglaise

Potatoes : Château and Boiled   Green Peas

Chapon à la Washington

Sweets:

Pouding Soufflé, Rothschild

Pears Caroline   Almond Macaroons

Savoury: Anges à Cheval

Dessert   Coffee

February 5, 1922

MUSIC

Overture . . .
"Mirella"   ...   Gounod

Waltz . . .
"Alsacienne"   Cassado

Selection . . .
"Iolanthe"   ...   Sullivan

Entr'acte . . .
"Chanson Triste"
Tschaikowsky

the end, the preference was given to the 1840. My Bacchante was quite a success, and Belcher hired a marvellous Chu Chin Chow costume from the Barber, suitable to his bulk, and looked simply screaming – in fact won 1st prize.

Of course it has been very hot the last few days, passing over the line [Equator]. I haven't minded it. We've got a big electric fan in the cabin, and I wrested the top bunk from Archie, and we sleep with no clothes on, and trust to Providence to wake up in the morning before the steward comes in! But the heat nearly kills poor Mrs Hiam. It's getting cooler again now.

With a lot of pushing, Sylvia Hiam is 'getting off' with young Ashby. He's such a nice boy, and she's the only young thing on the ship, but although very pretty, is a terrible mutt.

I have succeeded in talking to Mrs Blake, and find her most amusing. She dined at our table on the occasion of the last brace of the King's pheasants! Mr Murray, the commissioner, is very nice too. She is going to the Mount Nelson Hotel also, to be about three weeks with her father, who lives out there for his lungs, I gather. She and I have taken rather a fancy to each other.

To our intense surprise, Archie and I succeeded in winning the 2nd prize for Deck Quoits – and very nearly won the 1st prize. We selected very nice table napkin rings with the Kildonan Castle Arms on them. At one moment, I rather fancied I might win the Ladies singles, but there came against me, Mrs Fichardt, who is quite my idea of the Mother of the Gracchi, a great big fair woman, very calm, with really rather a statuesque figure built on big lines, no nerves, and about fourteen children who cluster round and urge her on in eager Dutch.

Mulandi

RHODESIA

CONGA MT. Cangombe LOVALE Lungo Soba Gaué Matongo
Gongo Kambutu Sitanda Matimba
Caconda Cangamba Cahuhue Kabompo Layinga MANICA Zamb
Shilembe Semalembues MENO
Ambuellas Lialai Monze Matua Chibing
Moi Katiba Nalolo ZAMBESIA Mwemba Maghauba
Damba M. Miango Salimao Namieta Sioma LIVING- BANYAL Inyungo
Gaseine M. Malome Gonye STON
Gold Mines Falls Victoria Sapatani RHODESIA
Handa Bavik Nona Falls Falls Wankies
Humbo Mpashi Linyanti MAKALA
Mai-Inis Daka Shangani R. Maka
Omondonga ONDONGA Okavango Sekumbwas Tama Malisa Zili eld
OVAMBO LAND SOUTHERN Kama Kama
Etosha L. RHODESIA Zouga Salt Pans Buluwayo
Okondju Otjituo Moremi
Otyzondyopat Omarumba L. Ngami Tati Lahombo
Omborombonga Ghanse Shasha R. rockodil
Otyimbinde R. Biles Pool
Okozondye Otyimbinde BAMANGWATO
OMATAKO MT. WINDHOEK KALAHARI Shoshong Pietersbur
Otyimbingue Gobabis Twass Maraba
kopmund Salem SOUTH Molopolole TRANSVAA
h Bay Rehoboth BAKUENA Kanye Nylstroom
ndwich Hoachanas DESERT Zeerust Middelburg Lyde
Harbor WEST Molopo R. Mafeking Rustenburg PRETORIA
OLLAM Gibeon Vryburg Lichtenburg burg
BIRD I. AFRICA Potchefstroom Heidel- Standert
(BR.) Beersheba Bloemhof berg
Spencer Bay Keetmannshoop Taungs Heilbron Utree
ICHABOE I. Kuruman Vaal Vryheid
ngra Pequena KARA Gobasti Koopman ORANGE Bethlehem Ulune
MTS. GRIQUA LAND Kimberley FREE Ladysm
Baker Bay Bethany Nisbet Griqua Griqua STATE NATAL
Orange River Bath T. WEST Bloem- Maseru P
Gariep GR. Hope T. fontein BASUTO
Port Nolloth O'okiep BUSHMAN Philippolis LAND Kokstad
Springbock Fn. LAND Smithfield Aliwal din
Hondeklip Bay Rosseveld Carnarvon CAPE OF Colesberg STORM John
Victoria Hanover GOOD OF HOPE Middelburg
Calvinia W. Richmond Tarkastad
Olifant River MTS. GOOD Beaufort W. Cathcart Soutterheim
Clanwilliam Fraserburg NIEUWVELD MTS. Murraysburg Somerset Beaufort King Williams T
Piquetberg UNION Peddie
Malmesbury Tulbagh Somit Uniondale Grahams
Stellenbosch Robertson CAPE COLONY Great Fish River
CAPE TOWN Paarl Caledon Swellendam Alexandria Port Elizabeth
Cape of Good Hope Melville Georgetown Cape St. Francis
False Bay Bredasdorp Mossel Bay
Cape Agulhas Riversdale

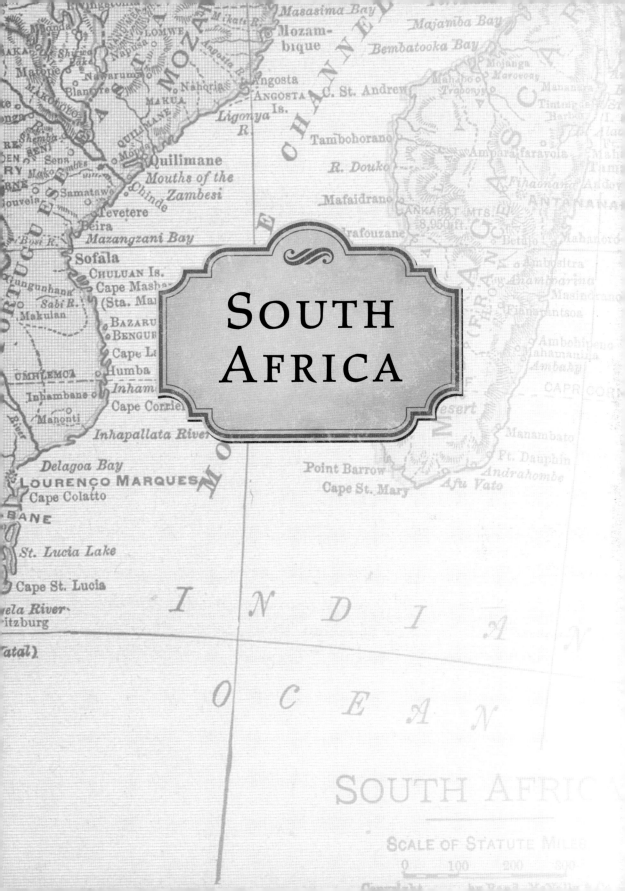

SOUTH
AFRICA

Luncheon

✠

TO MEET THE

BRITISH EMPIRE EXHIBITION
DELEGATES.

The Guests of . . .

The British Manufacturers' Representatives' Association
of South Africa (Incorp.)

Hout Bay Hotel,
8th February, 1922.

My memories of Cape Town are more vivid than of other places; I suppose because it was the first real port we came to, and it was all so new and strange. Table Mountain with its queer flat shape, the sunshine, the delicious peaches, the bathing – it was all wonderful. I have never been back there – really I cannot think why. I loved it so much. We stayed at one of the best hotels, where Belcher made himself felt from the beginning. He was infuriated with the fruit served for breakfast, which was hard and unripe. 'What do you call these?' he roared. 'Peaches? You could bounce them and they wouldn't come to any harm.' He suited his action to the word, and bounced about five unripe peaches. 'You see?' he said. They don't squash. They ought to squash if they were ripe.'

It was then that I got my inkling that travelling with Belcher might not be as pleasant as it had seemed in prospect at our dinner-table in the flat a month before.

This is no travel book – only a dwelling back on those memories that stand out in my mind; times that have mattered to me, places and incidents that have enchanted me. South Africa

meant a lot to me. From Cape Town the party divided. Archie, Mrs Hyam, and Sylvia went to Port Elizabeth, and were to rejoin us in Rhodesia. Belcher, Mr Hyam and I went to the diamond mines at Kimberley, on through the Matopos, to rejoin the others at Salisbury. My memory brings back to me hot dusty days in the train going north through the Karroo, being ceaselessly thirsty, and having iced lemonades. I remember a long straight line of railway in Bechuanaland. Vague thoughts come back of Belcher bullying Bates and arguing with Hyam. The Matopos I found exciting, with their great boulders piled up as though a giant had thrown them there.

At Salisbury we had a pleasant time among happy English people, and from there Archie and I went on a quick trip to the Victoria Falls. I am glad I have never been back, so that my first memory of them remains unaffected. Great trees, soft mists of rain, its rainbow colouring, wandering through the forest with Archie, and every now and then the rainbow mist parting to show you for one tantalising second the Falls in all their glory pouring down. Yes, I put that as one of *my* seven wonders of the world.

We went to Livingstone and saw the crocodiles swimming about, and the hippopotami. From the train journey I brought back carved wooden animals, held up at various stations by little native boys, asking threepence or sixpence for them. They were delightful. I still have several of them, carved in soft wood and marked, I suppose, with a hot poker: elands, giraffes, hippopotami, zebras – simple, crude, and with a great charm and grace of their own.

We went to Johannesburg, of which I have no memory at all; to Pretoria, of which I remember the golden stone of the Union Buildings; then on to Durban, which was a disappointment because one had to bathe in an enclosure, netted off from the open sea. The thing I enjoyed most, I suppose, in Cape Province, was the bathing. Whenever we could steal time off – or rather when Archie could – we took the train and went to Muizenberg, got our surf boards, and went out surfing together. The surf boards in South Africa were made of light, thin wood, easy to carry, and one soon got the knack of coming in on the waves. It was occasionally painful as you took a nose dive down into the sand, but on the whole it was easy sport and great fun. We had picnics there, sitting in the sand dunes. I remember the beautiful flowers, especially, I think, at the Bishop's house or Palace, where we must have been to a party. There was a red gar-den, and also a blue garden with tall blue flowers. The blue garden was particularly lovely with its background of plumbago.

Finances went well in South Africa, which cheered us up. We were the guests of the Government in practically every hotel, and we had free travel on the railways – so only our personal trip to the Victoria Falls involved us in serious expenses.

February 6 [Monday]

We have arrived! Great excitement as to whether we should get in today or not. The Chief Engineer had us into his cabin after dinner, and handed round Van Dams(?) (liqueurs), drinking several himself, and then became most suspiciously loquacious for one so Scotch, lamenting the fact that the Kildonan should be late on her first voyage. Between a fine of £100 for every hour she is late after 6 am and the fear of what the Board will say if he uses too many hundred tons of coal, the poor man is torn asunder. He then spoke movingly against early marriages, and besought Sylvia not to contract one rashly. We thought he must have been unfortunate himself, but it turned out that he was devoted to his wife, but pitied her deeply for being married to him!

We ran into a fog in the afternoon, and stayed about hooting dismally, but at last it cleared and we got in about 7.30 – just in time to have a lovely view of Table Mountain in the setting sun. A representative of the Union Government came on board to meet us, also the Deputy Trade Commissioner, Major Featherston. He had cars waiting for us, and had arranged for our baggage to pass straight through the customs without being examined, and we came right up here. Comfortable rooms and bath, indifferent food, and no one ever answers the bell unless it is by accident but then they are quite kind.

Tuesday [February 7]

Very hot. I love it but the Hiams are nearly dead again. The
Mountains all round make this place beautiful, and as you go
down to the town, there are the most lovely flowers climbing up
the houses, lots of mauvy *blue* ones, great morning glories and
a kind of blue hawthorn hedge. The men had to go to a lunch
so we went into the town to get films developed etc, and bought
a 1/ basket of peaches, great yellow ones, five we thought, but
discovered there were lots underneath and really about fifteen.
We ate them juicily in the garden, and little Natal pineapples at
2d each. I had begun to think that places where fruit cost next
to nothing only existed in books, but we have struck it here
all right. We learnt afterwards that 15 peaches for a 1/ was an
imposition, but I am still too fresh from London to be able to

The Mount Nelson Hotel.

feel it! I do wish you could be here. We would have a lovely eat together! Darling Mummy, it would be nice.

In the afternoon, I met Archie at the station and we went to Muizenberg, and surf bathed with planks! Very difficult. We can't do it a bit yet. But it was lovely there, with a bay of great mountains coming right down to the sea. I had no idea there were so *many* mountains. And the sea is *really* hot, the only sea I have ever known that you don't shiver when you first put your toes in.

Poor Belcher had a very bad foot – blood poisoning – its been getting worse all the voyage because he won't rest it. It keeps breaking out – rather like Archie's did. I'm very sorry for him. We're being taken on a motoring tour by prominent Manufacturers today. I do love this sunshine.

Agatha surfing at Muizenberg.

I sent you a cable and got yours about an hour afterwards. It is nice to know all is going well. I will write to Mr Rotherham about buying me another Chinese Bond. I like them! Undoubtedly this is a lovely trip. The only serious thing is, there seems to be no boat running to Ceylon. They all go to Bombay. It will be terribly sad if we have to miss it out.

This letter is for all, so send it on to Punkie. Love to her and James, and my own darling little Pussy Cat, and love to dear old Mont, and lots to you, darling. I will send some post cards and snap shots by next mail. Am not quite at home on the little Corona yet, as you may note, but at any rate its better than my handwriting! Keep well, darling, I wish you were here.

Your loving

Agatha

Agatha and Ashby.

Sea Point.

Mount Nelson Hotel
Cape Town

Wednesday February 8

We were treated to a long lecture by Belcher this morning. He began by saying that his doctor had expressly stated he was not to be thwarted or crossed in any way, that his blood pressure was abnormally high, and that any undue excitement would probably end fatally – which would be disastrous for the Mission, as no one else had a grain of administrative capacity. It was therefore absolutely necessary that the other board members of the Missions should do their bit with Featherston and shield their Chief. If they preferred to murder him instead, he fancied the thanks of the civilised world would be theirs!

Agatha in the pool at Sea Point.

Groote Scuur interior.

Mr Hiam spent the morning in the cold storage chambers, and came back with a solemn warning to us all never to eat any more meat whilst in South Africa! The fish here is uneatable anyway, and Belcher gave us a lurid description of what the natives do to the fruit – so it would seem that we must resign ourselves to slow starvation.

The Hiams went off to see some friends this afternoon. Quite a relief. Mrs H. is most kind and sweet, but a little stupid. It is really quite a puzzle sometimes to know how to go on talking to her.

Belcher took a car, and he and I and Archie drove out to Groote Scuur, Rhodes's house, where Smuts lives when he is here, and we went all over it. Most attractive, with the big Dutch wardrobes and cupboards, and the teakwood panelling. The bathroom is rather famous, all marble, and the bath hewn out of a solid block of granite. But the bath is too black looking to be attractive. There is a wonderful slope of hydrangeas in the garden, but they are over now. We went on to the Rhodes Memorial, and then Belcher tried to photograph the lions, offering the keeper the following tariff:

For making the lion turn its head round – 1/

For going into the cage – 2/

For sitting on the lion's back – 10/ (paid in advance)

The man replied with scorn that he looked after the birds and had nothing to do with the lions!

The Rhodes Memorial.

*Archie on the Rhodes
Memorial.*

*'Physical Energy',
Rhodes Memorial.*

Thursday [February 9]

Today is grey and cold. The Hiams rejoice, but I regret the heat.
Sylvia, I, and the Naval Attaché (Ashby) went off to Muizenberg.
High tide and shelving beach. I didn't tilt my board up enough,
and consequently it stuck in the sand, and jolted me violently
in the middle! I at once loathed surfing! But recovered shortly.
Ashby was rather good for a first attempt. Sylvia doesn't bathe,
in case she should get sticky! She snapped us both as we came
out 'resting on our boards', and suddenly a perfectly strange
young man bust up, raised his hat, said to me: 'may I have the
pleasure also?' and before I could reply, 'snapped' me neatly,
murmured 'Many thanks' and retreated again.

Archie came out after lunch, stayed in an hour, and got
very angry, because he didn't get one good run! It was awfully
funny to watch him trying so hard, and wave after wave passing
him by.

In the evening we went to the Town Hall, were received by
the Mayor and Mrs Gardiner, and had a lovely concert which
we heard from their box. The conductor, Wendt, is as good as
anyone I have ever heard.

The faithful Featherston (whom Belcher persists in referring
to as Wetherslab) returned with us. We were instructed in
a fierce whisper to remain in the lounge, and not to suggest
going up to the sitting room, in the hope that he would leave
sooner. But Wetherslab seemed quite happy, drank soda water
in small sips, and pointed out five elderly gentlemen in turn, the

formula being the same. 'You see so and so? Sir Harry Whatnot. Rich, but quite second class. You wouldn't care for him at all.' One by one the members of the Mission strolled away to bed, followed by murderous glances from Belcher who had given strict orders that he was *not* to be left alone with Featherston. The last I heard was F. saying: 'You see that fellow sitting behind you?' Bel. 'Not having eyes in the back of my head, I don't.' F. (quite unperturbed) 'He's the Governor's A.D.C. Quite your sort. I'll bring him up.' Bel. 'You'll do nothing of the sort. I won't meet anyone tonight – first class, second class or third class!' F. (sympathetically) 'I expect you do get fed up with the kind of fellows you meet out here.' I should not be at all surprised to learn tomorrow that (a) Featherston's corpse had been recovered in the garden or (b) that Belcher had succumbed to an apoplectic fit!

[Friday] February 10

Darling Mother

I can't in the least remember where I left off! And whether I told you about our day out with the British Manufacturers Representatives? They came for us with cars and took us out for a whole day's motoring, over the 'neck' of Table Mountain, through lovely pine trees down a winding road to Camp's Bay on the other side, and all along the coast road on the side of the mountains – just like Hope's Nose and the New Cut at Torquay! (No matter where Millers go, they always say it is just

like Torquay! But it *is*). We had lunch at Hout's Bay – a most attractive Hotel with big shady trees growing up through the floor of the 'stoep' which I always disgrace myself by calling the verandah, and we ate at long tables under the shadow of the trees. I had Archie on one side (they put all husbands and wives next to each other) and a Mr Oldfield on the other side, and we had a most delightful conversation about vaccines and dog ticks! Belcher made an excellent speech.

Then we drove on, through Constantia to see the vines, which I mistook for young tomato plants for some time! Fields of them, standing about 2ft high, like little currant bushes. We passed orchards of peach and pear trees also.

We had tea at the Majestic Hotel at Kalk Bay, and came home through Wyneberg, where most of the Cape Town people seem to live, and through Rhodes Avenue, where great oak trees meet overhead in an arch for about a mile or so, past the natural Zoo where Spring bok and Wilde beast (spelt wrong) [sic] walk

Lunch at Hout's Bay, from left to right: Agatha, Archie, Mrs Edwards, Mr Edwards, Major Featherston, Mrs Hiam, Mr Brown and Mr Hiam.

about, with some lions and baboons in cages, and saw the Rhodes Memorial in the distance on the hill side. Young Ashby was with us, and at that moment delivered himself of the innocent remark: 'Rhodes? That was the fellow who died quite rich, wasn't it?'

Belcher is becoming very irritable. I don't wonder really for his leg and foot are quite bad, bursting out in new places. The doctor says he must lie up and rest it, and he says he can't afford the time. Bates had forgotten to get him more carbolic, and he'd had a tight boot on all day, the food in the hotel was atrocious, and the doctor has cut him down to one whiskey and soda a meal, so matters nearly reached a climax last night! Also, he is getting very fed up with Major Featherston, who attaches himself to Belcher like a faithful dog, and comes up at all hours of the day and night. He runs downs South Africa incessantly, apologising to us for the 'second class' people – 'Not like *my* friends in New Zealand.' In fact, we gather that the *only* first class people in South Africa are Prince Arthur of Connaught ('I see a lot of him, of course') his A.D.C. and – Major Featherston! He tells us all about his clothes, and the terrible duty he had to pay on 'the half dozen 16 guinea suits I brought out from England – of course one can only get second rate stuff out here!' However, he bent to pick up a handkerchief today, and Ashby, to his great delight, discovered a large patch of foreign material in the seat of the immaculate one's trousers, and came to tell us the glad news in great glee. We all feel much better in consequence.

Saturday [February 11]

The industrious and perspiring Bates wrestled all yesterday to erect the B.E.E. models in the Chamber of Commerce, and this morning Sylvia and I went down to see them and afterwards tried on a lot of hideous hats in the town to recuperate after the strain of talking intelligently about them to the inevitable Wetherslab, and a red faced man called Archie Simpson, who was one of our hosts on the motor drive, on which occasion, he nearly drove Belcher into the Indian Ocean and frightened him to death.

This afternoon Archie and I went to a place beyond Muizenberg called Fish Hoek, and bathed. It's the only place one can swim round here, either its surf bathing like Muizenberg, or else they have large tanks on the beach washed by every tide in which you feel rather like a fish in an aquarium! This was a lovely little place ringed round with mountains, white sand beach, and about six little white bungalows on the mountain

Archie in the sand dunes at Fish Hoek.

side. No bathing huts (and no cover!) but a kind young man offered us a hutch where he kept fishing tackle, and we had a delicious bathe. Nevertheless, swimming is a little tame after surfing! We are going to buy light curved boards (that don't jab you in the middle) and absolutely master the art. Archie loved Fish Hoek, of course, and would much prefer staying here to going up to Rhodesia. It is amusing after the crowded beaches in England to come to a place where when there are ten people and three children on the beach, you hear someone murmur: 'How terribly crowded it is today!'

Sunday [February 12]

Today a selection of us went out to call on the Admiral at Simonstown, Belcher having lunched with him yesterday. B. wanted to take Archie and me, but we agreed that that would hardly do, so I and Sylvia Hiam went with him and had a most pleasant time. Lady Goodenough has been ill and looked very frail, but was quite charming, and the Admiral is a jolly old boy, and took me all round the garden and showed me his ponies, and insisted that Archie and I must come out and lunch one day before we left Cape Town and I must bring my camera and take some views. He has two quite cheery daughters, one not out yet. The flag lieut. had an eye for me, I think – but the Admiral gave him no chance.

I fear Ceylon is quite off now. There are no boats from here – they all go to Bombay, and the Ormuz which we are trying

to catch, touches at Colombo but not at Bombay. So we are
cancelling the passages, and sailing direct for Australia from
here somewhere about the 30 March, I expect.

As this was mail day, posting this to catch up.

Love to all, Agatha.

*Archie, Admiral,
Lady Dorothy, Lady
Goodenough and their dog
Simon at Simonstown.*

MOUNT NELSON HOTEL
CAPE TOWN

February 15 [Wednesday]

Dearest Mummy

The Hiams are a strange family! Neither Mrs Hiam nor
Sylvia are enjoying this trip in the very least – but are longing to
get back to England. The heat tries them, there is so much dust,

the houses are so Dutch looking and unEnglish, the food is bad (true!) and (like Mrs Gummidge) if a mosquito bites them, it is worse for them than for other people – they feel it more! Then why come? I gather that Mr Hiam owns and farms the greater part of East Anglia. His father was a yeoman farmer in a rather large way, and the son conceived the brilliant idea of being the man who sold his father's potatoes in London, with the result that he is worth just over a million. And yet, when you can afford to travel all over the world regardless of cost, you don't enjoy it! As a matter of fact, *he* does – but only because of comparing the farming and agriculture generally, but still he is cheerful and always pleasant. I suppose it is rather dull for the girl. She's a bit too young to enjoy any intelligent sight seeing, and there aren't any dances or picnics or young peoples' shows, and she is simply counting the days till she can get back to England. I find an evening spent with Mrs Hiam rather trying. She asks so many questions. I forget if I told you, but she said four times the other day what an extraordinary thing it was that there should be a Llandudno and a Clifton in South Africa 'Just the same names as in England!' I hinted that it was a phenomenon fairly often encountered in our colonies, but she repeated 'Actually the same as in *England*' and seemed to think it was a clear case of thought transference! They are quite attached to me. I iron their clothes for them, tell them what trams to take in the town to get back to the Hotel, and deal and shuffle for them when we play cards, neither of which accomplishments they can master!

Half holiday today! Archie came back from Muizenberg boasting that he *can* surf at last! Nobody believes him! But he rambles on while at the same time Hiam and Bates explain how *really* they practically got to the top of Table Mountain. Nobody believes them either, and Bates branches off earnestly to describe a particularly vicious looking spider that blocked his path, and how he distinctly heard a snake hiss. Bates has been convinced ever since leaving England (which he has never left before) that he is going into deadly peril and will never return alive. He insisted on the B.E.E. insuring his life before he started! Madeira he eyed askance as being full of pirates, and when a shark was seen at sea, it was sure to be Bates who saw it. Belcher has told him that there are young leopards on Table Mountain, and he believes it. We sent him a P.C. yesterday with a picture of a Puff Adder on it, and an earnest warning purporting to come from the 'Society of the Protection of Visitors' and Bates has been busily looking them up in the Telephone Directory, and cannot understand why no one seems to know where their offices are!

Thursday [February 16]

Yesterday afternoon, Mrs Blake and I went to the museum where we met two cousins of hers, one a *very* pretty girl, Marye Cole, who has been a great success with the Connaughts and others out here, and the other a Mrs Thomas who lives in Italy but has come out here to lecture on art. She dug out the head of the Museum and made him show us round. They have models from life of all the various Bushmen tribes, some of which are now dying out – extraordinary little women with enormous behinds trained out in a point! He explained them all very interestingly, and then we went on to the rock carvings and paintings done by prehistoric people. (Just like the reindeer ones, Punkie.) He showed how they were not just a lot of odd animals grouped together, but actually represented a particular hunt or drive. One eland's legs look all out of drawing, but if you look closely, you see a tiny red spot, and the hunter indicated sketchily behind is holding a red tipped arrow, so you realise that the animals legs were supposed to be broken and that is why it is 'all queer'. Most of the beasts have white foam coming out of their mouths, but one has red, and is sinking to the ground evidently dying. All the animals were finished minutely, but the hunters are very sketchy, and that is supposed to be on account of the superstitious idea that some tribes still hold – that it is unlucky to make a likeness of anyone – like the Egyptians wax figures. All the carved animals were begun the same way, from the round of the stomach, and if they saw the beginning had gone wrong, they abandoned it and began again.

He then gave us a very interesting lecture on all the early skulls of which they have models, from the Pithecanthropus downwards. A chimpanzee's skull is beside it to show that the Java man was *not* a man, but a walking ape. Then the Piltdown, with a man's brain, but very pronounced ape teeth, and the Heidleberg jaw, very ape like, but with quite modern human teeth, the Neanderthal people, with their enormous queer shaped heads, but still with straight jaws and quite unable to

articulate speech, and the negro type which shows that Africa, as well as Europe, passed through the Neanderthal phase of evolution, and a lot about the African skull, and how stupid the people who dug it up were, and lost a bit of the eye socket which was most important and prevents them from reconstructing it properly. At the end you come to various types of 'bushmen' African and Australian. There is one African type that is very interesting to me, because it is so extraordinarily different from all the rest, long from the back to the front and flat on top, just like the Neanderthal type – and so on down to the modern European, and in the end one realises that there is really very little difference in the *head*, but an enormous difference in the *jaw* and jaw angle. It was altogether one of the best afternoons I have ever spent!

Adderley Street,
Cape Town.

Drying fruit.

This morning we started at 9.30 (actually at 10.15 as Belcher wasn't ready, having lost his temper over being kept 35 minutes waiting for his breakfast in the dining room, after having taken the trouble to be up and down by eight. So he marched out in a fury, and said he wouldn't have any breakfast, and about an hour later was attacked by the pangs of hunger and the reflection that anyway the Hotel wouldn't care whether he went without breakfast or not!) and started on a tour of the principal Fruit Farms. First to the Mallesons' at Ida's Valley where we arrived about 11.30. Mrs Malleson was an enormously stout woman in an ancient blue print dress which was burst in three places down her ample back, but who was quite charming and rather like old Ma Lucy. We went in for 'tea' which you always have here in the middle of the morning. All the Dutch houses are alike, delightfully low and cool and dark. It's so funny to want dark rooms after always wanting 'bright' ones in England. We had tea and tomato sandwiches and hot buttered toast, and delicious melons, with pears, peaches and plums to fall back upon, and then went out to see the Fruit which after it is picked is cooled and when it is well cooled down is packed for England, or else is taken into a hot place and ripened for drying. When ripe, the peaches and plums are cut in half and peeled with just a little cap of skin left on the back for it to dry into, washed, sterilised by being put into a stone chamber with burning sulphur. Then the great wooden trays are laid out in the sun, and when it's finished it goes to a factory to be processed and pressed into a good shape.

Mrs Malleson is very keen on water lilies, and has some beautiful blue ones which are supposed to be very rare. I liked her very much and found out in the end that she is a niece of the Strubens, and that the Strubens themselves are supposed to be arriving at this hotel shortly.

Lunch at Pickstone's Farm.

Mr Pickstone (left) and Mr Hiam with the vines at Rhodes fruit farm (right).

We left about 1 o'clock and drove on over the mountains to the Pickstones, who farm on a larger scale. A lovely house, with vines and grapes hanging down all along the stoep, and inside a sort of moorish court with arches and two great pomegranate trees on the green grass enclosure. We had an excellent lunch served by two smart maids, old glass on the table, and lovely old Dutch furniture everywhere. It is a beautiful spot, right in the midst of the mountains. About 3 o'clock we went on to the Rhodes Fruit Farm, and were taken over it by the Manager. I was by then rather weary of seeing fruit dried, it's the same everywhere, and it was scorchingly hot. The Hiams were so done to the world that they wouldn't get out of the car, Sylvia thought she had got a touch of the sun, and Mrs H. was exhausted with the strain of holding on her hat (having no motor veil)! Also, as they explained, they felt the dust more than most people! I wanted to see the fruit canned – quite interesting. When the tins are filled with fruit and syrup they run along a little moving platform through a tunnel of steam, come out the other end all hot, a machine claps the top on, and the sealed tin falls into a big vat of boiling water and is cooked. We also did a tour of the vineyards, and tasted some of the wine – just pure fermented grape juice, the people they send it to turn it into port or sherry or whatever they think most suitable. I never knew that. I always thought that port was port from the start! We had tea with the Manager's wife, and then home along a still dustier road, which the Hiams felt very much!

Rhodes Fruit Farm.

Row A   No. 3

OPENING OF PARLIAMENT

20th JANUARY, 1922

17 FEB
SECOND SESSION, FOURTH PARLIAMENT

Admit *Mrs Christie*

to the SENATE GALLERY, on the occasion of the Ceremony of the Opening of the Second Session of the Fourth Parliament of the Union of South Africa, in the Senate House, Cape Town, by His Royal Highness the Governor-General and Commander-in-Chief, on Friday, the 20th January, 1922, at Noon.

17, FEB,

MAURICE GREEN,
Gentleman Usher of the Black Rod.
[P.T.O.

Friday [February 17]

Today was the opening of Parliament to which we went dressed in our best. The three ladies had very good seats in the front of the gallery and saw beautifully. Prince Arthur read the speech very well, and the Princess looked almost nice for a Royal, all in white with a mushroom lace hat. The speech which was of some length was read again in Dutch when it seemed interminable! In the afternoon more bathing at Muizenberg, and we bought surf boards with curved ends – much easier and less painful, and I believe one could have great fun with them at Paignton on a rough day.

Everyone in South Africa seems to be called Van der Byl or Cloete. I suppose Charles sprang from here originally!

Mount Nelson Hotel, Cape Town

Postmark: Feb 18 1922

We motored round here yesterday. Love from both. AC

Saturday [February 18]

The Archbishop's garden party today, of which I enclose an account with description of myself in the 'Ponting' frock we bought together. Archie and I represented the Mission. A lovely garden, right up by the mountain, terraces of flowers, nearly all blue (Feb. is the 'blue' month, so Mrs Malleson told me). There was a square 'rose garden', another blue agapanthus garden, and a scarlet lily garden, also a water garden where the water came down in steps with different coloured water lilies. Mrs Malleson (who had discarded her blue print for very smart black satin in which I nearly failed to recognize her) showed us round. Princess Arthur looked a terrible dump in hot dark blue and red. The first person we saw as we got in was the Admiral in an immense white toupee who confided to us that he had just come from the golf links and that he hated this kind of show.

In the evening, Archie, Belcher and I dined with Mrs Blake, and the attractive Marye Cole (who is really very like a young Gladys Cooper). Nigel Battine, the Flag Lieut. completed the party, and afterwards we motored out to Wynberg where there was a dance on. I enjoyed myself enormously. Battine, who is quite an amusing youth with no mean opinion of himself, confided to us that the Admiral had worn the wrong hat at the garden party, and that he feared there would be trouble about it in the morning! The correct one with plumes was to have been sent up to meet the Admiral at the golf links, but by a regrettable oversight 'someone had blundered'! The Duke of Manchester's son, Lord Mandeville was at the dance, and seemed to be rather a friend of Marye's who ordered him about freely under the term of 'Mandy'.

GARDEN PARTY AT BISHOPSCOURT.

Archbishop and Mrs. Carter "At Home."

A WOMAN'S VIEW.

(By MAB.)

SOME PRETTY DRESSES.

An English visitor, Sir Percy Stothert, was, with Lady Stothert, who wore a beautiful frock of pale-grey accordian-pleated georgette, which had a softly-draped bodice and handkerchief draperies over the skirt. A smart cerise plume trimmed her brown hat. With them was Mrs. W. Felloes Morgan, an American lady who knows how to wear her gowns. She wore black charmeuse, draped with a wide hip sash and touches of orange georgette flecked with gold on bodice and sleeves. Her small toque was of brown beaver velour. Mrs. A. Christie, who is visiting South Africa with her husband, a member of the British Empire Exhibition Mission, looked lovely in pale yellow beaded on the bodice with steel beads and a big black bow and ends on the left hip.

Sunday [February 19]

A day of peace, as Belcher went off in a car at 9.30 to spend the day at some Minister's estate. Hiam and Mrs Hiam (the latter somewhat reluctant, correctly suspecting another Fruit farm in disguise) accompanied him. Belcher has been really terrible lately, rushing about like a mad bull, confusing everybody, wanting impossible things done, and displaying manners equal to those of Kipling's Sea Cow! After lunch, Archie, Bates and I started out to ascend Table Mountain. It was lovely going up through the pine woods, but after that it is all loose stones and very tiring, although it's a regular track and not actual climbing at all. I soon abandoned the party. Bates was striding ahead like a tiger, but he too failed before he quite got to the top, so Archie alone scaled the heights. We were all very stiff and went to bed early.

Monday [February 20]

A most enjoyable lunch with the Admiral. Belcher was in a vile temper all the morning, and despatched a telegram to say he had missed his train, so Archie and I went alone. The Goodenoughs are really awfully nice. Col and Lady Dorothy Meynell were there, staying with them, and Lord Mandeville, and we had a most cheery lunch. They wanted us to stay on, and motor to Cape Point, but duty called! We took some snapshots of the house from the garden and went down to the pier from which they bathe, and Lady G. looking down into the water said quietly: 'Ah, I see the Octopus has gone. Such a fine fellow – about 5ft across.' We bathed from the other side of the pier. I never care to bathe close to an octopus!

They suggested a foursome at golf when we return to Cape Town. They really are quite dears. Will send you some of the snap shots if they come out all right.

Tuesday [February 21]

Played bridge with Dr Gordon (Belcher's doctor) and his mother last night. They have a most delightful dog. His name is Joe! A smooth haired fox terrier, well bred, and with the same delightful eagerness of manner that makes our Joey so fresh and attractive. When commanded he chases his tail, going round and round, and suddenly pausing in triumph with it firmly clamped between his teeth! Then he goes out of the room to 'hide his eyes' while a piece of biscuit is hidden and then tears in to look for it. He is extraordinarily fond of playing with fire, and they daren't leave him alone with a fire in the room. He pulls all the wood off, singeing his whiskers and growling fiercely, and as soon as a match is lighted by anyone for a cigarette he makes a spring for it – like Joe for a buzz buzz.
A charming person!

The mail will be in this morning. I hope I shall hear from you or Punkie this week. There was nothing last week. It is definitely settled now that we sail for Adelaide on the Aeneas on April 7th from Cape Town. The Hiams are going earlier, on the Sophocles, and we meet again in Adelaide. I am glad to be rather longer in South Africa. It is so nice and hot, and Australia will be rather cold. We are lunching at Government House today.

Lots and lots of love, and to dear old Mont.

Your loving

Agatha

Letter came from *you* – I must compose a few inspired words for Punkie!

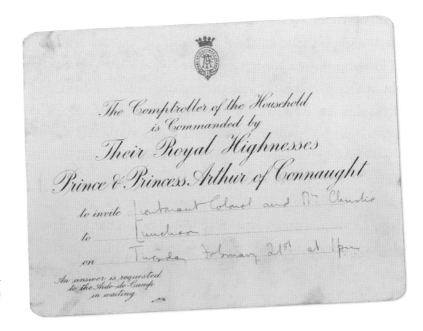

Invitation to Government House.

Tuesday, February 21

Darling Mummy

Lunch at Government House today. We arrived there and were received in the hall by a little A.D.C. who showed us a plan of the luncheon table and where we were to sit. Then we were announced and went into the drawing room where the Prince and Princess and a lot of other people were assembled. (Sylvia was by then petrified with fright!) A terrible five minutes ensued during which the Princess and I tried to keep up a conversation. She is known throughout South Africa as being only capable of saying 'oh, yes.' Then lunch was announced and the Prince and Princess stalked in and we followed. I sat at the Princes's right, with Mr Malan, the Minister of Mines, on my other side. Belcher and Archie were either side of Her Royal Highness. The other Ministers there were Burton, the Finance Minister, and his wife, and Sir Thomas and Lady Smartt, and Mr and Mrs Jagger (Minister of Railways) and a lot of nice A.D.C.s and of course the inevitable Wetherspoon (next to Sylvia). I enjoyed talking to Malan immensely, we wandered through the topics of public speaking, concerts, conducting and conductors, famous preachers, the mistakes made in writing lives of great men, and he talked very interestingly about mines and strikes. The Prince was pleasant, but rather a stick until nearly the end of the meal when he suddenly brightened up and asked me if I knew 'Why

Mr Malan, Minister of Mines.

the Queen dislikes Lord Lascelles?' The answer being 'Because he pinched her little Mary' and continued: 'I know a good many more about Lascelles, one very good one – but I'm afraid its quite unrepeatable!' I urged him on but he shook his head and remarked 'Not *now* at any rate, but I'll tell you this much, its supposed to be a telegram from the Jockey club congratulating him.' He then proceeded to the safer ground of a definition of an optimist as 'a man who runs away with someone else's wife.'

A small rather ill bred Selleyham incommoded our feet, and begged persistently. When biscuit and cheese time arrived, the Prince produced a biscuit and said: 'Now he shall do his trick ask for it!' Needless to say, as always when shown off, the royal dog displayed the usual obstinacy and incompetence, and his master was left explaining that usually he did it perfectly!

Belcher and Archie got on heroically with the Princess, and quite cheered her up. Belcher told her his famous lion story, and she and Archie agreed that they both hated getting up early and could never remember people's names, to which Archie added cheerily 'But that must be rather awkward for you in your line of business.'

The men remained behind to discuss the B.E.E., and in the drawing room Lady Evelyn Farquhar, the lady in waiting, came and sat down by me, and proved most entertaining. I gather she lives and breathes for shooting, and started by condoling with me heartily on the fact that shooting in Rhodesia would not begin until May. She herself has just bought some land in the Transvaal where she intends to have a farm. 'No animals – just fruit and things, and of course there's lots of shooting round there. My girls love it, go around in a shirt and shorts – not that

HRH Prince and Princess Arthur of Connaught.

I ever wear shorts myself. I find slacks every bit as comfortable!' she was a most refreshing creature.

Two elderly ladies advanced on Sylvia and led her to a distant window seat, giving her the cheerful information that they were the two oldest wives of Prime Ministers in the country, Sylvia, who has no overwhelming affection for the elderly, and who had been listening entranced to my racy conversation with Lady Evelyn, went most unwillingly.

The Princess has quite nice fair hair, which she has just bobbed, and her neck and arms are burnt blacker than anyone I have ever seen.

Afterwards we motored out with Dr Vander Byl to see an explosive factory, and wandered about there amongst super phosphates and detonators. A lovely spot, by a lake in the midst of the mountains.

Friday [February 24]

Nothing of much interest of late. It's very much hotter and we go and lie in a 'pool', a sort of open air sea swimming bath at Sea Point, about ten minutes by tram from Cape Town. Grand crisis last night. The Union Government has given us free passes and a saloon on the Railways, but Rhodesia has been pig headed and would only dole out three passes, and declined to have our saloon running over their lines without payment of 1/4 a mile (which would work out at about £140) and as the Hiams are off going to Rhodesia, fearing heat and malaria, possible sleeping sickness and certain mosquitoes, this rather tore things. The ultimatum arrived last night, and Belcher flew into a really magnificent rage, and after a few preliminary remarks as to its being everybody else's fault for not handling the Railways properly, proceeded to draft and send off vitriolic telegrams, Bates taking them down in shorthand, typing them out and dashing off to the P.O. with them in a taxi, and returning to do it again as Belcher thought of fresh things to say. He wired to the Administrator, to all the Rhodesian newspapers, to every conceivable official, and the burden of them was all the same, 'I'll be ---- if I'll go near your ---- country now' put into slightly politer language.

Our itinerary (for the ninth time) was again completely revised by the perspiring Archie, and we are now leaving by R.M.S. *Briton* for Durban on Tuesday next, and working through the Transvaal from there. As we don't do Rhodesia, we shall probably get off by the Sophocles with the Hiams.

Saturday [February 25]

A day at the Kenilworth races. Archie, Bates and I formed a 'little syndicate' (as you can't put on less then 10/) 4/ for me and A. and 2/ for Bates. But we did not do well. The GG. [the Governor-General, prince Arthur] was there and the Admiral who suggested a day's golf – but our plans are too chaotic at the moment to make any plans. I shouldn't be at all surprised if we didn't go on the Briton after all. I fancy Belcher is a little worried as to whether he has gone too far in his telegrams to Rhodesia.

Sunday [February 26]

Lunch with Sir Abe Bailey at his house at Muizenberg. He is quite an old dear. There were a lot of people there. I sat next to one of the A.D.C.s and enjoyed myself very much. It is a very nice house – also built originally for Rhodes. We met Mrs Blake afterwards and surfed! Splendid waves.

Monday [February 27]

Mail in today. *Good* Mummy! Horrible Punkie. My darling little Rosalind – its just the time that she got a sort of bronchial cold last year, and Nurse was awfully good then, never wanted

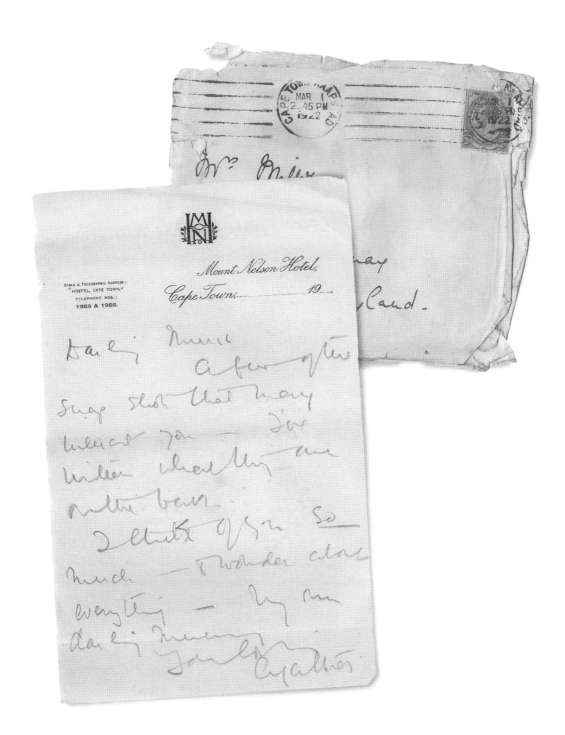

to go out or anything and didn't mind how much she was sick. My little Teddy.

Very glad you've got an invalid chair for Monty. Remember I have 200 in my deposit at home if you want it. Cable me and I would cable Rotherham. I feel rather awful being away enjoying myself and living on the fat of the land here.

Lots of love to you all
Your loving
Agatha

Rhodesia has climbed down utterly, will do anything we want! Great success of Belcher's fierce tactics. Grand revising of the itinerary, everything being now fixed up for Durban. I think we shall do that first and Rhodesia afterwards, returning here to catch the Aeneas on the 7th April.

MOUNT NELSON HOTEL
CAPE TOWN

Postmark: Mar 1 1922

Darling Mummy

A few of the snap shots that may interest you – I've written where they are on the back.

I think of you so much – and wonder about everything – my darling mummy
Your loving
Agatha

"Lion Head".
Capetown.

...n bedroom

...
& "Betty"
...Capetown

March 8 [Wednesday]

Darling Mummy

A most strenuous time of travelling. Archie, Mrs Hiam left Cape Town on the boat for Durban – a terrific south easterly got up, so I decided to go with Belcher and Bates by train. We stayed in our saloon on Wednesday night at eight o'clock – it was the hottest day I have ever known. Table Mountain seemed to get red hot and radiate it down, and you just breathed red hot dust. Mrs Black has spent the whole of the afternoon lying in the pool at Sea Point. She is going home by the Arundel on Friday and has given me her address, we are going to see each other in London.

The first night in the train was quite all right. When I woke up the following morning we were in the Karroo, all dust and stones and tiny bushes and little hills, rather wild looking and desolate – and attractive from that point of view – but it got steadily hotter and hotter till the train was like an oven or a peach house in Summer. Belcher and I played piquet most of the day and drank lemon squashes without ceasing!

Once the sun goes down it is quite cool again, we got to Bloemfontein early the following morning when the Hiams joined us, having come up from East London. Bloemfontein is not much of a place, very flat and an ugly town. In the afternoon the Secretary of the Agricultural Union took us out in a car

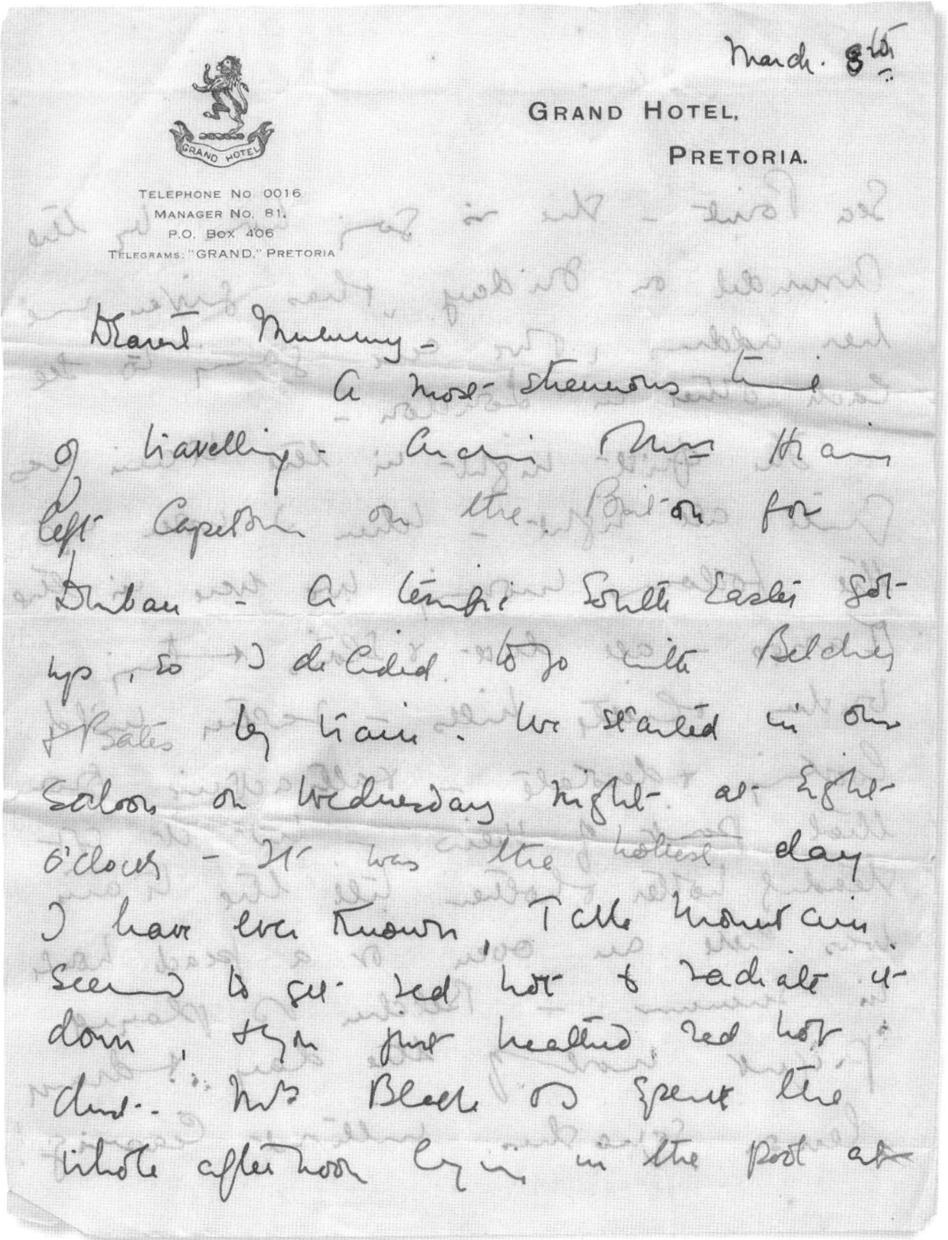

March. 8th

GRAND HOTEL,
PRETORIA.

TELEPHONE No. 0016
MANAGER No. 81,
P.O. Box 406
TELEGRAMS: "GRAND," PRETORIA

Dearest Mummy -

A most strenuous time
of travelling. Our train
left Capetown with the Baileys for
Durban. A terrific South Easter got
up, so I decided to go with Belcher
& Bates by train. We started in our
saloon on Wednesday night at eight
o'clock - It was the hottest day
I have ever known. Table Mountain
seemed to get red hot & radiate it
down. Sky just beltend red hot
dust. Mrs Black & spent the
whole afternoon lying in the pool at

and we saw over the Bloemfontein Creamery and then on to a Government farm run by Major Quin. We had tea there with his wife and their daughters and a Mr and Mrs Helm (?) [sic] and their three lovely children (one a girl of four, so like my Teddy! She insisted on being dressed up in flowers by one of the Quinn girls and she showed herself off saying, with great satisfaction, I am a servant girl!!) The Helms have gone out to live in South Africa for two years as he has suffered so terribly from asthma. He is a water diviner and we all tried and it works with me a bit too! Very exciting? Major Quinn told us of an old man who must be well over a hundred and knew Bloemfontein when it was only one house owned by an old farmer called Bloem. When asked how old he is, the old man draws himself up proud and says, 'I was born before the days when men began to *count* their years!' (with intense scorn).

The following morning we left at 9.15 a.m. for Harrismith, rather lovely scenery in the afternoon all through the hills – rather like Dartmoor round Two Bridges. We got to Harrismith about midnight, but slept in train which was shunted on to sidings and went to the Hotel for breakfast. I discovered, before leaving the train, that my camera was missing. Must have been pinched from the compartment by someone whilst we were in the dining car. I'm very upset over it, luckily I *did* insure it before leaving, but they cost more out here.

Harrismith is a charming little place, about 6000 feet up with rolling downs and a nice fresh breeze. We were taken on a long motor tour over the veldt to see various farms all owned by members of the de Jaeger family, some of whom could speak English and some only Dutch.

On Monday we took the 2.15 p.m. train and arrived at Durban the following morning at 7 o'clock, a glad reunion with Archie! Belcher had been charming on leaving Cape Town, but at Bloemfontein General Hertzog had refused point blank to meet him, and his temper suffered in consequence, also a new B.E.E. pamphlet, supposedly written in Afrikaans turns out to be in High Dutch. The wretched Bates was nearly slain in consequence. In fact, he was officially dismissed and told he could return to Southampton at once by the first boat, but the sentence appears to be commuted to separation from the High War Lord, to be attached to Archie and myself for Johannesburg and Rhodesia. Belcher is not going to Rhodesia, he is returning by the *Briton* to Cape Town and sailing on the *Sophocles* if he can get through in time. But Archie in fear he won't and that we shall have him with us on the *Aeneas* after all!!

Our little American friend, Mr Mayne, was at Durban and took us out in his car to a place where the gardens are full of blue monkeys who come and help themselves to your tea. Durban is lovely, very tropical looking –

Your loving
Agatha

(Will send rest of this letter later. Strike on, and mail is uncertain)

Other letter continued…

[undated]

but (like all really beautiful places) just like Torquay! When you
drive along the 'Berea' you might be going along the Warberry's.
It made me feel quite homesick.

Having arrived at 7.15 a.m. I departed with Archie for
Johannesburg at 5.50 in the afternoon. We arrived about 5
o'clock the following day.

At Germiston a wire was handed in from the Trade
Commissioner at Joburg (Major Langton) saying Joburg
was unsafe, he would meet us on the platform there and had
arranged accommodation for us at Pretoria instead. We arrived
and he and his wife met us. All the Hotels had shut down that
afternoon with their waiters etc. on strike and there was no
meat and no bread, as the bakers had come out. The strikers had
stopped all taxis and pulled out the drivers. They were throwing
hand grenades in the street. They had got hold of a private car
for us, with an R.G.F. officer who has gone home, and we took
what luggage we could and bundled ourselves in.

Major Langton had got two passes for us, one (if held up
by strike commandos) saying it was our private car, that A. was
in the Offices of Imperial Army and nothing to do with Union
Government and the other if the Government people held us
up. And when our chauffeur had laid a large automatic in a
convenient place, we walked off feeling quite excited. But no one

interfered with us and I've reached here all right. Today they have proclaimed martial law in Joburg and all the bars are shut here. It seems all idiotic for coming here to try to talk about an Exhibition that is to be held in two years' time, but we are off to Rhodesia on Tuesday, so must do what we can. They don't think the Railways will come out, and this place is pretty quiet.

    Lots of love to all

        Yours

           Agatha

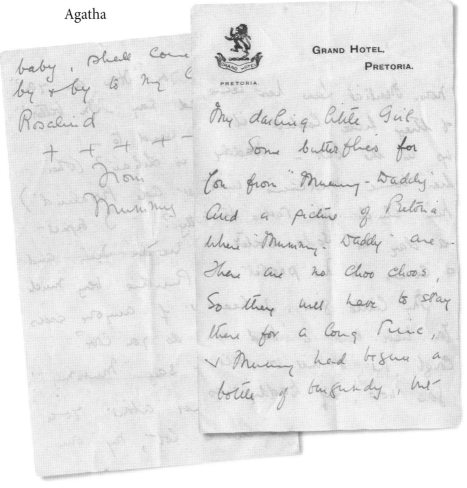

[undated]

My darling little girl

Some butterflies for you from 'Mummy–Daddy'. And a picture of Pretoria where 'Mummy–Daddy' are. There are no choo choos so they will have to stay there for a long time, Mummy had brought a bottle of burgundy, but now Martial Law has come and they have locked it up in the bar. Daddy has some medicine with him which he takes twice a day in soda water and carries it in his pocket.

My little girl, I hear you have had a 'bad cough', but it will be all gone now, and if Daddy was to ask you 'How are you?' you would say 'I'm better!' like you used to.

How is Lilian? (Then focus 'just ask Rosalind') And Betty? I suspect you love Uncle Jim and Auntie Punkie very much now, but if anyone asks you 'Who do you love?' you must say 'Mummy'!

I think about you such a lot, my own baby, I shall come back by and by to my little Rosalind.

x x x x x x x

From

Mummy

Church Sqr, House of Parliament, Pretoria.

Postmark: Transvaal 15 Mar 22

On our way to Rhodesia from Pretoria this morning. AC

CHURCH SQR. HOUSE OF PARLIAMENT PRETORIA.

D. J. MAHONEY, MANAGER.

P.O. BOX 231.   TELEGRAMS: "SAVOY."   TELEPHONE 293.

Kimberley, March. 15.

L. DAVIS, PROPRIETOR.

Darling Mum—

I sent my last letter in
two halves since the last part of it was
about strike, & everything was being censored—

We were in Pretoria from ~~Tuesday~~
Wednesday to the Tuesday following — Once
there, we couldn't get away again,
the strike having turned into a
young revolution — they hoisted
a red flag & proclaimed a Soviet
Government — One body of the Police
was cut off out on the Veldt &
surrounded by the rebels & they
fought for 48 hours when our
aeroplanes discovered them & got
ammunition & food to them until
they were relieved — Two aeroplanes
were shot down—

Of course Pretoria was quiet
enough — we had martial law there
& armoured cars dashing up and
down & could occasionally hear
bombs in the distance — Miss
Wright (whom I met on the boat)

March 15 [Wednesday]

Darling Mum

I sent my last letter in two halves since the last part of it was about strike and everything was being censored.

We were in Pretoria from Wednesday to the Tuesday following. Once there, we couldn't get away again, the strike having turned into a young revolution. They hoisted a red flag and proclaimed a Soviet Government. The body of the police was cut off out on the veldt and surrounded by the rebels and they fought for 48 hours. Then our aeroplanes discovered them and sent ammunition and food to them until they were relieved. Five aeroplanes were shot down.

Of course Pretoria was quiet enough, we had martial law there and armoured cars dashing up and down and could occasionally hear bombs in the distance. Miss Wright (whom I met on the boat) teaches in the University there and was very nice to us. We swam together in the open air baths and went to Bridge with her. Mainly all her students are Dutch and being Nationalists, in sympathy with the strikers. On Saturday we heard that Smuts had arrived having dashed through the rebel lines and with his tyres shot to pieces. They arrested 1500 students that night, so we thought that all might be over, but on Sunday battles were raging closer than ever. There were still no trains running at all from Johannesburg.

Union Buildings, Pretoria.

Mrs Harvey (the wife of the Industry man who was looking after us) took us over the Union Buildings one morning. They are rather wonderful architecture, with two lovely moorish columns and fountains. We saw Smuts' room and old Kruger's chair, and then Mr Venn, the Under Secretary for the Interior, took us down to the archives and showed us a lot of interesting old documents, including the first treaties of the Dutch with Dingaan in Natal. Also the peace signatures in the Boer War.

Mr Blundell, Under Secretary for Industries, and his wife motored us out to the Country Club for tea on Sunday. We just got back before the daily thunderstorm, which occurs punctually at 5 o'clock.

Matters were getting desperate for Rhodesia, and we worried Harvey again on Monday, but they refused us permits to leave Pretoria, as the road between there and Johannesburg was unsafe, a large commando hovering about in the vicinity. The railway line was torn up, I fancy, as no trains were leaving Pretoria, but we heard that they were going try and run a train through to the Cape from Johannesburg and taking Rhodesian passengers round by Bloemfontein as there seemed no hope of returning direct to Mafeking.

However, on Tuesday morning, having arrived round while I was still in bed, with permits for us to leave and a government car would be round in twenty minutes. Frenzied toilet and

Across the ampitheatre (above left) and the view from the pavilion of the Magelsburg Range (above).

Kimberley.   packing! We just took suitcases, all we could cram in, and left trunks with Bates who is to rejoin Belcher at the Cape as soon as a train runs. Had a splendid run into Joburg, stopped once or twice by cheerful looking city gentlemen, smoking pipes, with bayonets tucked rakishly under their arms.

Our train was due to leave at 10.45 and it got off at 11.30 to the sound of artillery and shrapnel as the great attack on Fordsberg, which was to end the war, was just beginning.

We got to Bloemfontein at 11 last night, slept there, and started on here 9.15 'this morning', arriving at lunch time. Our proper train left last night, of course, so we have to wait until tomorrow evening and shall arrive at Bulawayo Saturday

morning. I was terrified I was going to miss the Falls after all with this strike trouble, as we have to get back to Cape Town by the 7th.

Very hot and dusty here, and just as the diamond mines are all closed down at present.

I'm having all letters kept at Cape Town while we are on these wild wanderings.

Lots of love to you, darling Mum, to Monty. I suppose you are at Torquay now.

Your loving

Agatha

18 March [Saturday]

Dearest Mother

We spent an interesting day at Kimberley seeing over De Beers. None of the mines are working now, and they don't expect them to for another year at least, as no one is buying diamonds, but we saw all the pits, and the washing machinery, and the wired in compounds where the natives live. One native had a bad abscess on his leg once, they treated it and treated it, but it wouldn't heal, and at last they operated and cut it open, and found a parcel of diamonds inside wrapped up in a dirty rag! If the rag had been clean, he would have got away with it very likely! We saw a lot of rough diamonds being graded, they are far more glassy and less pebbly than I thought, and also some show ones cut, a most lovely deep orange one worth £500 a carat, that is the most expensive colour, then blue, white, and ordinary yellow is the commonest.

We left for Bulawayo on Thursday night. Friday was quite an interesting day passing through Bechuanaland [Botswana], (although the dust pours in and nearly chokes you!) as at each station there are crowds of natives with funny carved toys, and patchwork fur rugs and beads and baskets. Lady Goodenough had quite a collection of them on a little table, and they really are rather fascinating. We bought more than will be easy or convenient to pack, but some people called Thompson, next

OPPOSITE:
Selling bowls.

Bulawayo to the Cape

AMC
Buying Animals!

AC
Sugar Canes for Sale

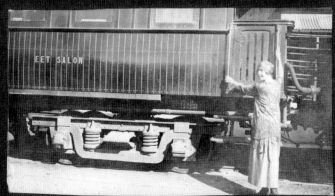

Agatha entering the "Eet Salon"
(Lunch time!)

Buying Animals. Archie.

door to us, far outdid us, and their carriage is simply snowed up with spotted leopards and native warriors! They are rather amusing people, fairly ordinary, but enjoying themselves so tremendously that it is quite refreshing after the Hiams! We got to Bulawayo Saturday morning after a disturbed night. At 3 a.m. an exquisitely dressed young man, looking like a musical comedy hero of the Wild West, entered our compartment, and asked Archie where he was going. Disregarding Archie's first murmur of 'Tea – but no sugar in it', he repeated his question, laying stress on the fact that he was not a waiter but an immigration officer. Archie, still fast asleep, replied: 'Australia – at least, no, I'm going to Salisbury first.' At last we succeeded in satisfying the gentleman that we had no infectious diseases, were visiting the Administration, and gratified him with A's christian name, place of birth etc. and he withdrew. Endeavoured to snatch a little sleep, but were aroused again at 5.30 by the arrival of the liquid sugar known as coffee, dozed

Agatha at the Matoppos.

till 6 when tea full of sugar arrived, at 6.30 proper tea came, and after it we fell asleep exhausted, to awaken just outside Bulawayo with none of the animals packed! Bulawayo is not very attractive, flat and sandy and a dirty Hotel full of smells. After lunch we had a car and drove out to the Matopos. That was wonderful, great boulders strewn about and piled up in fantastic shapes, as though giants had been playing. Four great sets of these boulders surround Rhodes' grave. It's a wonderful place to be buried, in the midst of a giant's playground! In the thirty miles between it and Bulawayo, there is only one habitation halfway, a kind of Hotel where we had tea. Archie went to pay for it, and found the proprietor digging placidly in the garden, and evidently quite new to his trade of Hotel keeping for he murmured, 'You say you've had cake and jam, I fancy that's 1/6 – now is that 1/6 each, or for the two?' We start tonight for Salisbury, arriving there 6 tomorrow evening.

Monday [March 20]

Arrived last night. This hotel is like a super Town Hall to
look at, and is very comfortable. The Administrator, Sir
Drummond Vhap Chaplin, is away, but Mr Montagu, the acting
Administrator, and his sister, are living in the Hotel, and she
took me out with her in her car this morning, and we saw the
town, and Government House, where Lady Chaplin keeps quite

*Mr and Miss
Montague.*

Archie in his Rhodesian hat among the paw paws.

a menagerie, aviaries full of birds and owls a lot of monkeys, and eland and zebras. Also three white Aberdeens, who were being groomed, each by his own 'boy'! Lady Chaplin has two dogs, a cat, two cages of birds, a parrot, and a small monkey brought into her room every night to sleep! We returned to tea in Miss Montagu's room, with a Mrs Mackenzie, wife of the Attorney General, a rather pose lady, dressed in carefully thought out shades of pastel blue. Miss Montagu herself is charming. The Administrator Mr Hone, came to lunch which we had at the Montagu's' table. I had afternoon tea with them, and after it drove first to Mrs Douglas Jones, wife of the Resident Commissioner, and then to a piece of land which the Montagu's have bought, and where they have a great collection of flowering shrubs. The poinsettia hedges were lovely, but it was rather late for most of the other things. Also there is an orchard of mango trees, paw paw trees, bananas and avocado pears. They intend to build there one day, but he has been 25 years in Rhodesia, and doubts if he can stand the climate now that he is growing old.

Tuesday [March 21]

Spent a day in the Mazoe Valley Citrus Estate. Rhodesia is quite different to the rest of South Africa. It's all wooded slopes. The road down into the valley is rather lovely, you go through great sunflower crops, and then drop down through the woods to

Mazoe Valley, Archie with Mrs and Mr Swain.

the dam from which they irrigate the valley. Orange trees are very smart with their glossy leaves. We saw grapefruit also, and picked a large quantity of lemons to take with us on the train. We had tea with Mr Swain, the manager, and his wife and little girl, and their importunate dog, who displays a great yearning for cake and caresses and does much damage with his large tail. He appears to be a French bulldog which has grown to the size of a mastiff!

We had Bridge in the evening with the Taylors (he manages the Tobacco factory and is called Tobacco Taylor to distinguish him from another Taylor), and heard a lot about Gertrude Page, and Cynthia Stockly, the Rhodesian authoresses. The latter's daughter got engaged to an impecunious young man called Bunker Brown, but her mother vetoed the match, sent her daughter back to England, paid Bunker Brown's debts and married him herself!

BULAWAYO

Thursday [March 23]

I was very sorry to leave Salisbury. It was far more like England as regards the people, and I liked the Montagu's immensely. They were so nice to us. The last excitement was running over a snake in the car! A morning in Bulawayo which has been dusty and hot. We are just off to the Falls, where we shall arrive at the favourite South African hour of 6 am tomorrow morning.

OVERLEAF:
Victoria Falls

Monday [March 27]

It has been lovely here. I can't bear to leave. Its not just the Falls themselves, although they are very wonderful – especially the width of them, I didn't realise that they stretched for a mile and a quarter – but the whole place. No road, only paths, just the Hotel, and primeval woods for miles and miles stretching into blueness. A delightful Hotel, long and low and white, with beautifully clean rooms, and wired all over like a fine meat safe against malarial mosquitos. An urgent telegram arrived from Belcher telling us to return to Cape Town via Johannesburg and 'complete original programme' and demanding an answer by wireless, so he really has gone on the *Sophocles*, for which the Lord he thanked. We visited the rain forest, where the spray falls continually, and walked out to the Eastern cataract and met a Barotsi woman carrying two infants on her behind, and the whole of her household goods including frying pans on her head, whilst her fine looking husband walked ahead in a gay blanket!

On Saturday we went on expedition up the Zambezi, first by 'trolley' to the boat house (you never walk a step in Africa. The trolleys are pushed by perspiring natives. A swimming team was here and George Graves and his party, and they got gay and loaded up a trolley with about twenty and it ran away, and George Graves lost a finger and is in the Livingstone Hospital) then in a smart steam launch up the river. We saw a crocodile

'Never walk — take the trolley'. Agatha seated on the left next to Mrs Thompson, with Archie standing far left.

Agatha embarking on the launch on the Zambezi.

straight away, which cheered us very much. We landed higher up the other side, and were trolleyed to Livingstone, which boasts about six buildings and is the capital of Northern Rhodes. The Thompsons, who have arrived here, quite lost their heads buying curios, the final one being a two shilling tiger measuring 6 ft. We fell to two charming 'hippos' which Archie, who had to carry them, said weighed a ton at least! Back in the trolley, and by launch to Kandahar Island where we had lunch. Tea on another island and home. (A special canoe took back the Thompson's purchases.)

And now back at Bulawayo. I did hate leaving the Falls, and the Zambezi and the palms.

Our letters will be at Johannesburg.

Lots of love

Agatha

MOUNT NELSON HOTEL
CAPE TOWN

3 April [Monday]

Darling Mum

No news of any of you for a long time. I hope everything is all right?

Two splendid batches of press cuttings from John Lane were awaiting me here. Very good ones in 'Truth', 'Punch' and 'Bystander' which is nice. I think the dedication has made quite

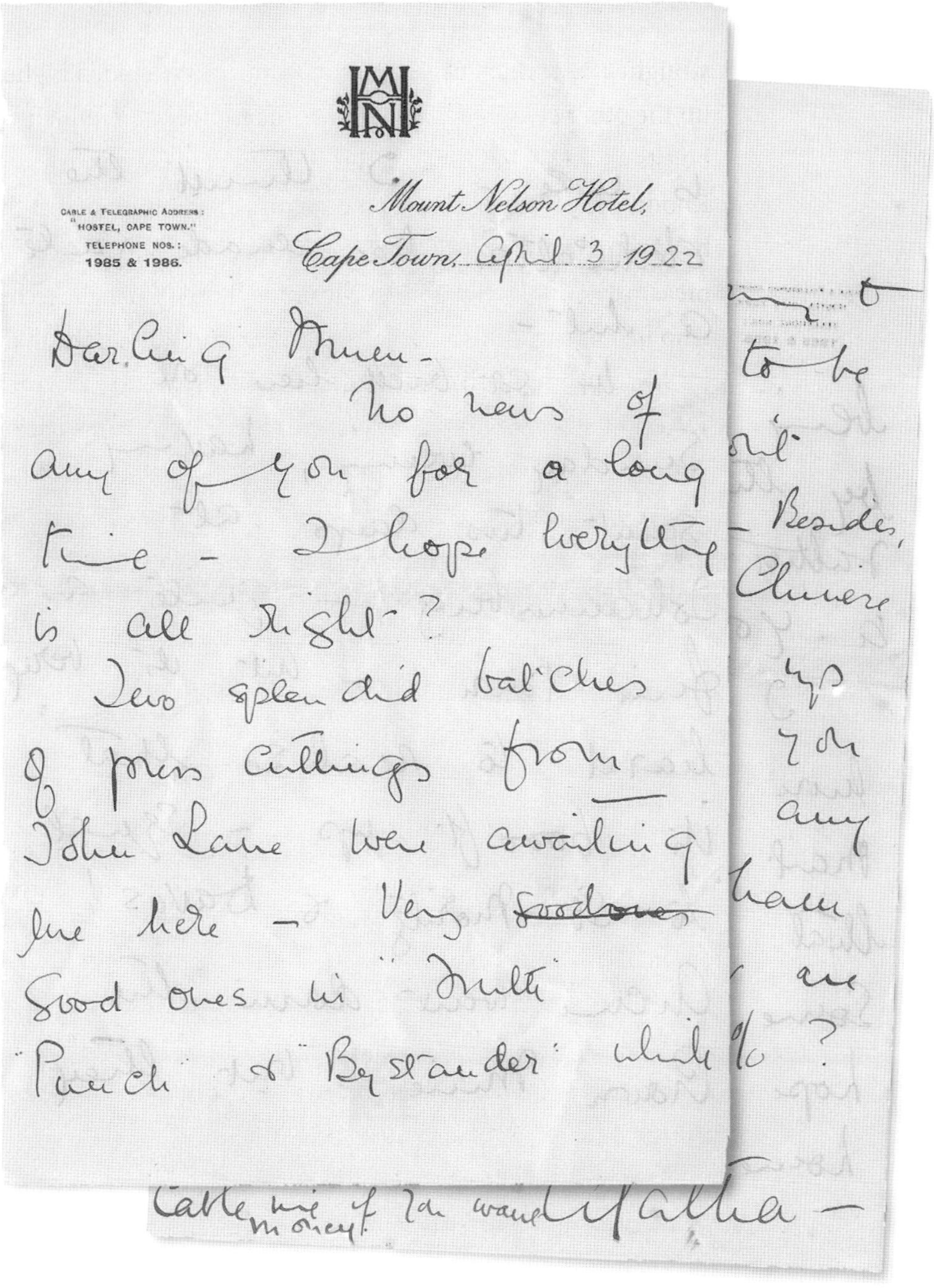

CABLE & TELEGRAPHIC ADDRESS:
"HOSTEL, CAPE TOWN."
TELEPHONE NOS.:
1985 & 1986.

Mount Nelson Hotel,
Cape Town, April 3 1922

Darling Muen —

No news of any of you for a long time — I hope Everything is all right?

Two splendid batches of press cuttings from John Lane were awaiting me here — Very ~~good ones~~ good ones in "Truth" "Punch" & "Bystander" while

Cable me if you want of other money —

a hit. ['*To all those who lead monotonous lives in the hope that they may experience at second-hand the delights and dangers of adventure.*']

We got back here on Sunday evening, having spent two days at Johannesburg, quite a fine town, but it is very hard to realise that it's 6000 ft up. Equal to St Moritz and Davos!

Archie went down the Crown Mine, but they wouldn't let me. Rather sad as I should have loved to have seen it. Gorgeous scenery coming down to Cape Town through the Hex River Pass. I've taken some photos of it which I hope will come out.

I've been very worried about my collection of wooden animals and how to get it home, but we picked up a very nice ex-naval man, Captain Crowther, on the train. He is out here for a 'paper firm' and presently it turned out that this was none other than Wilfred's! [Wilfred Pirie's firm.] Wasn't it funny? And Admiral Login he always called his 'Sea Daddy' – and also knows Geoffrey Watkin. He is taking our animals etc. home with him on Friday and will despatch them from Southampton to Torquay. Three cases in all. You needn't unpack them unless it would amuse you, but I think the one with the fur 'Kanorses' ought to be unpacked. I've had them put in a separate case. The little one is Teddy's 'fair covair' as she calls it, for her very own.

We sail on the *Aeneas* on Saturday [8th] for Adelaide. The 'wild man' may be there or may have gone on to Melbourne. Mr and Mrs Hiam have returned to England!! Mrs Hiam being completely broken up by the heat! And I rather fancy Sylvia has a young man in Cambridge.

I shall send you some more snap shots by this mail, I suspect after that you won't hear for some weeks. I shall hope to find letters from home waiting in Adelaide.

I really feel Tommy & Tuppence is going to be a success, so don't worry about money. Beside I've had two more Chinese Bonds drawn, look up your 5% ones if you have any and see if any were drawn – Rotherham will tell you. Or are yours all the 4½%?

Love to old Mont.

Yours

Agatha

Cable me if you want money.

MOUNT NELSON HOTEL
CAPE TOWN

April 3 1922 [Monday]

Dear Punkie

Do write. The only letters that arrive are Mrs Hemsley, William and Campbell [Archie's step-father and brother] – all my family might be dead. Write me about my baba. It's a *month* now without a word – the first three weeks I got letters from Mother. Also I want to know about Monty and everything, but especially my Rosalind. Tell her I have bought her a little 'fair rug' for her very own to go on her pram and a spotted giraffe made by black babas in Bechuanaland. I feel 'all queer'

OVERLEAF: *The Hex River Pass, picture taken from the back of the train as approaching curve, and the map from Agatha's collection.*

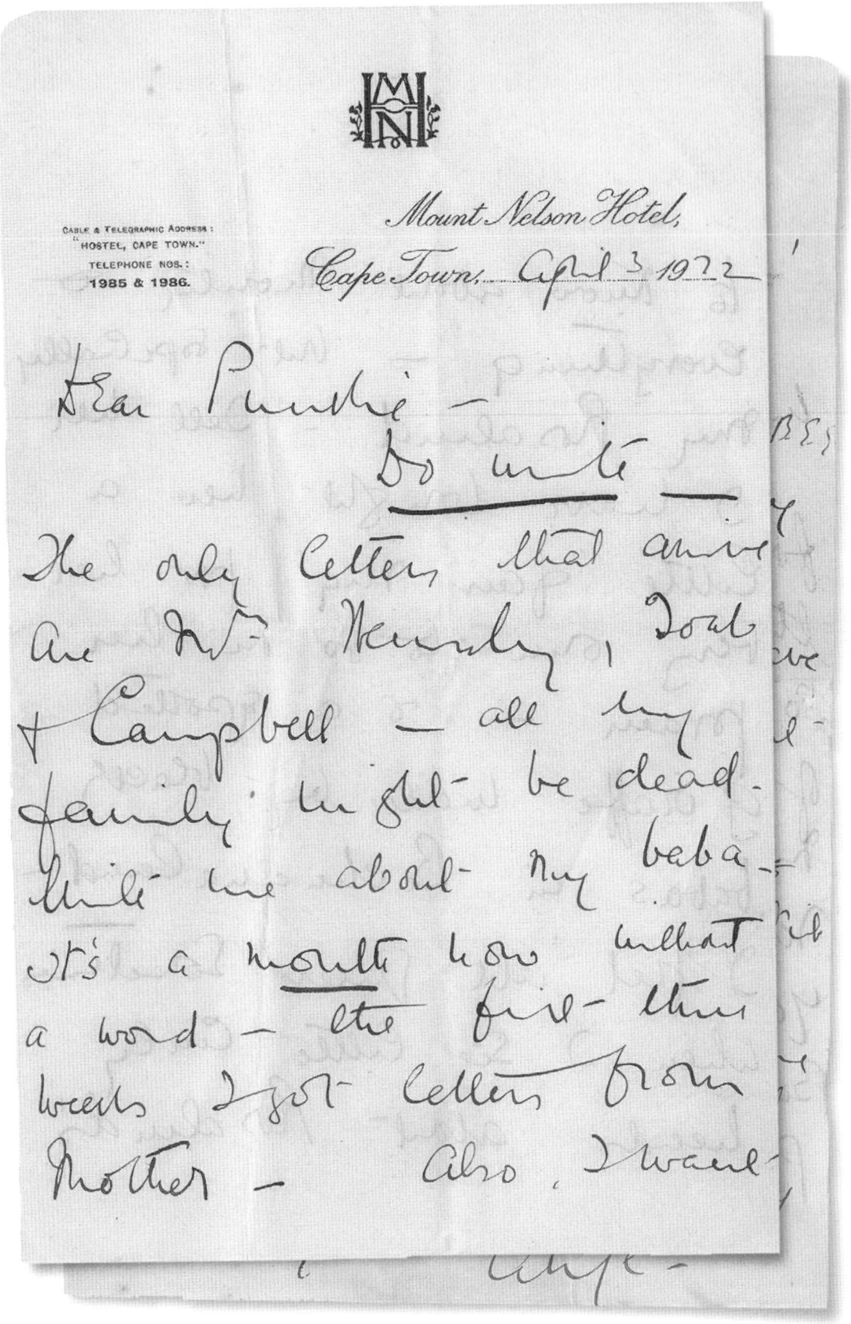

CABLE & TELEGRAPHIC ADDRESS:
"HOSTEL, CAPE TOWN."
TELEPHONE NOS.:
1985 & 1986.

Mount Nelson Hotel,
Cape Town, April 3 1922

Dear Punchie —
Do write —
The only letters that arrive
are Dr. Wernley, Toul
& Campbell — all my
family might be dead.
While we about my baba —
It's a month now without
a word — the five-three
weeks I got letters from
Mother — Also, I want

sometimes when I see little curly heads about Rosalind's size.

Two batches of press cuttings from John Lane, *all* good, not one bad one. I'm very pleased with the *Punch* one. It's lovely here, better than any other place in South Africa because of the bathing. Archie can stay in three-quarters of an hour here, and I could stay in two hours!! And no one hustles you in your bathing cubicle and they all have glasses!

We must come out one winter, Punkie. I believe it's only £38 Blue Funnel, and living fairly cheap and we would eat peaches and figs, and it really *is* hot! In fact Mr and Mrs Hiam have just gone home completely broken down with the heat.

Hasn't anything come for me? No grateful thanks from the people to whom I sent copies of the S.A. [Secret Adversary] (N.B. – Even my nephew has not responded!!) I'm cabling you to send on the Baggage Burglary Insurance Policy. It was due before we left, but hadn't come. So it would go on to you (you've got the address, haven't you – c/o B.E.E., 16 Hobart Place?) My camera was stolen on the train, the Co. here have paid up all right, but of course they ought to have seen the policy – and the next time they might not be so obliging.

Ask James if there are any stamps I can send him from Australia.

Do write me about my Rosy Posy.

Yours

Ange

OCEAN

Port Darwin
Clarence
PERON IS.
C..Hay
Darwin
Burrana
Union

Londonderry
Bougainville
Cambridge Gulf
Brunswick B.
Bigge I.
BUCCANEER ARCHIPELAGO
Ord Springs
LACEPEDE ISLES
Wyndham
Der
KIMBERLEY
Ord R.
Berdia R.

ROWLEY SHOALS
C. Baskerville
DAMPIER LAND
Fitzroy R.
WITTENOOM MTS.
NORT

C. Latouche Treville
Poissonier Pt.
Low Sandy Coast
SANDY DESERT
MT. MULLER
DAVENPORT RANGE

DAMPIER ARCHIPELAGO
NTE BELLO IS.
Cossack
De Grey R.
Barrow I.
North
est Cape
C.
har
Roebourn
Ashburton R.
GREAT SANDY DESERT
WESTERN
TERR

er I.
Gascoyne R.
Carvon
k
Hamlin Pool
Natta
TROPIC OF CAPRICORN
Weld Springs
Windich Springs
L. Augusta
AUST
Lake Amandeus
Kamaran Well
MUSGRAVE RANGE
C.

Wittenoom
Geraldine
Yum
Dunduindewa
A
GREAT
AUSTRALIA
VICTORIA DESERT
L. Cary
BLYTH RANGE
Ouldabinna
SO

reenough
Dongarra
McPherson
Grey St.
Bera Bera
Mingan
Two Springs
Ularring
AUS

Whitfield
New Norcia
Gnukadunging
Bardock
Kalgoorlie
Coolgardie
Paring Spring
NULLARBAR PLAIN
Kulna
Pelunibi
Pu
P
Pidin
Colo

PERTH
Fremantle
New Castle
York
Bora Yukin
Jarrahdale
Smith Sta.
L. Lefroy
Cowan L.
Yullarburra
Yayoudle
Dempster Sta.
Kaleuna
HAMPTON RANGE
Port Eucla
Ya

Pinjarra
Bannister
Williamsburg
Dundas Hills
Pontons Sta.
Pt. Culver
HEAD OF THE GREAT AUSTRALIAN BIGHT
Fowler Bay
NUYTS ARCHIPELAGO

Bunbury
Busselton
Brockman
Nyumup
Kojonup
Manjinup
Green Val.
Pollyenup
Wyndham
Albany
Tor Bay
Dundas Hills
Esperance Bay
EASTERN GROUP
RECHERCHE ARCH.
Flin

Australia

Farewell DINNER

GIVEN ON BOARD

T.S.S. Aeneas, Blue Funnel Line,

:: ON THURSDAY, APRIL 27th, 1922. ::

Commander - - - W. K. WALLACE.

From South Africa we set sail for Australia. It was a long, rather grey voyage. It was a mystery to me why, as the Captain explained, the shortest way to Australia was to go down towards the Pole and up again. He drew diagrams which eventually convinced me, but it is difficult to remember that the earth is round and has flat poles. It is a geographical fact, but not one that you appreciate the point of in real life. There was not much sunshine, but it was a fairly calm and pleasant voyage.

It always seems to me odd that countries are never described to you in terms which you recognise when you get there. My own sketchy ideas of Australia comprised kangaroos in large quantities, and a great deal of waste desert. What startled me principally, as we came into Melbourne, was the extraordinary aspect of the trees, and the difference Australian gum trees make to a landscape. Trees are always the first things I seem to notice about places, or else the shape of hills. In England one becomes used to trees having dark trunks and light leafy branches; the reverse in Australia was quite astonishing. Silvery white-barks everywhere, and the darker leaves, made it like seeing the negative

of a photograph. It reversed the whole look of the landscape. The other thing that was exciting was the macaws: blue and red and green, flying through the air in great clustering swarms. Their colouring was wonderful: like flying jewels.

We were at Melbourne for a short time, and took various trips from there. I remember one trip particularly because of the gigantic tree ferns. This sort of tropical jungle foliage was the last thing I expected in Australia. It was lovely, and most exciting. The food was not as pleasing. Except for the hotel in Melbourne, where it was very good, we seemed always to be eating incredibly tough beef or turkey. The sanitary arrangements, too, were slightly embarrassing to one of Victorian upbringing. The ladies of the party ware politely ushered into a room where two chamber pots sat in isolation in the middle of the floor, ready for use as desired. There was no privacy, and it was quite difficult …

A social gaffe that I committed in Australia, and once again in New Zealand, arose in taking my place at table. The Mission was usually entertained by the Mayor or the Chamber of Commerce in the various places we visited, and the first time this happened, I went, in all innocence, to sit by the Mayor or some other dignitary. An acid-looking elderly female then said to me: 'I think, Mrs Christie, you will *prefer* to sit by your husband.' Rather shame-faced, I hurried round to take my place by Archie's side. The proper arrangements at these luncheons was that every wife sat by her husband. I forgot this once again in New Zealand, but after that I knew my place and went to it.

We stayed in New South Wales at a station called, I think, Yanga, where I remember a great lake with black swans sailing

OPPOSITE: *Trees at Gippsland.*

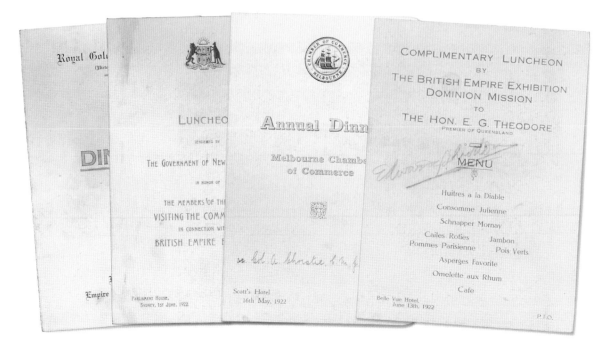

COMPLIMENTARY LUNCHEON
BY
THE BRITISH EMPIRE EXHIBITION
DOMINION MISSION
TO
THE HON. E. G. THEODORE
PREMIER OF QUEENSLAND

MENU

Huitres a la Diable
Consomme Julienne
Schnapper Mornay
Cailes Roties   Jambon
Pommes Parisienne   Pois Verts
Asperges Favorite
Omelette aux Rhum
Cafe

Belle Vue Hotel.
June 13th, 1922

P.T.O.

Dinner and lunch menus.

on it. It was a lovely picture. Here, while Belcher and Archie were busy putting forth the claims of the British Empire, migration within the Empire, the importance of trade within the Empire, and so on and so forth, I was allowed to spend a happy day sitting in the orange groves. I had a nice long deck-chair, there was delicious sunshine, and as far as I remember I ate twenty-three oranges – carefully selecting the very best from the trees round me. Ripe oranges plucked straight from the trees, are the most delicious things you can imagine. I made a lot of discoveries about fruit. Pineapples, for instance, I had always thought of as hanging down gracefully from a tree. I was so astonished to find that an enormous field I had taken to be full of cabbages was in fact of pineapples. It was in a way rather a disappointment. It seemed such a prosaic way of growing such a luscious fruit.

Packing pineapples for the market at Beerburrum.

The Russell River,
Babuda, Queensland.

Part of our journey was by train, but a good deal of it by car. Driving through those enormous stretches of flat pasture land, with nothing to break the horizon except periodic windmills, I realised how frightening it could be: how easy to get lost – 'bushed', as the saying was. The sun was so high over your head that you had no idea of north, south, east or west. There were no landmarks to guide you. I had never imagined a green grassy desert – I had always thought of deserts as a sandy waste – but there seem to be far more landmarks and protuberances by which you can find your way in desert country than there are in the flat grasslands of Australia.

We went to Sydney, where we had a gay time, but having heard of Sydney and Rio de Janeiro as having the two most beautiful harbours in the world, I found it disappointing. I had expected too much of it, I suppose. Luckily I have never been to Rio, so I can still make a fancy picture of that in my mind's eye.

It was in Sydney that we first came in contact with the Bell family. Whenever I think of Australia I think of the Bells. A young woman, somewhat older than I was, approached me one evening in the hotel in Sydney, introduced herself as Una Bell, and said that we were all coming to stay at their station in Queensland at the end of the following week. As Archie and Belcher had a round of rather dull townships to go to first, it was arranged I should accompany her back to the Bell station at Couchin Couchin and await their arrival there.

We had a long train journey, I remember – several hours – and I was dead tired. At the end we drove and finally arrived at Coochin Coochin, near Boona in Queensland. I was still half asleep when suddenly I came into a scene of exuberant life. Rooms, lamp-lit, were filled with good-looking girls sitting about, pressing drinks on you – cocoa, coffee, anything you wanted – and all talking at once, all chattering and laughing. I had that dazed feeling in which you see not double but about quadruple of everything. It seemed to me that the Bell family numbered about twenty-six. The next day I cut it down to four daughters and the equivalent number of sons. The girls all resembled each other slightly, except for Una, who was dark. The others were fair, tall, with rather long faces; all graceful in motion, all wonderful riders, and all looking like energetic young fillies.

It was a glorious week. The energy of the Bell girls was such that I could hardly keep pace, but I fell for each of the brothers in turn: Victor, who was gay and a wonderful flirt; Bert, who rode

Burt and Victor Bell.

splendidly, but was more solid in quality; Frick, who was quiet and fond of music. I think it was Frick to whom I really lost my heart. Years later, his son Guilford was to join Max and me on our archaeological expeditions to Iraq and Syria, and Guilford I still regard almost as a son.

The dominant figure in the Bell household was the mother, Mrs Bell, a widow of many years standing. She had something of the quality of Queen Victoria – short, with grey hair, quiet but authoritative in manner, she ruled with absolute autocracy, and was always treated as though she was royalty.

Amongst the various servants, station hands, general helpers, etc., most of whom were half-caste, there were one or two pure-bred Aborigines. Aileen Bell, the youngest of the Bell sisters, said to me almost the first morning: 'You've got to see Susan.' She does the most wonderful imitations.' So a bent, aged Aborigine came along. She was as much a queen in her own right as Mrs Bell in hers. She did imitations of all the girls for me, and of various of the brothers, children and horses: she was a natural mimic, and she enjoyed very much doing her show. She sang, too, queer, off-key tunes.

'Now then, Susan,' said Aileen. 'Do mother going out to look at the hens.' But Susan shook her head, and Aileen said, 'She'll never imitate mother. She says it wouldn't be respectful and she couldn't possibly do a thing like that.'

Aileen had several pet kangaroos and wallabies of her own, as well as large quantities of dogs, and, naturally, horses. The Bells all urged me to ride, but I didn't feel that my experience of rather amateurish hunting in Devon entitled me to claim to be a horsewoman. Besides, I was always nervous of riding other people's horses in case I should damage them. So they gave in, and we dashed round everywhere by car. It is an exciting experience seeing cattle rounded up, and all the various aspects of station life. The Bells seemed to own large portions of Queensland, and if we had had time Aileen said she would have taken me to see the Northern out-station, which was much wilder and more primitive. None of the Bell girls ever stopped talking. They adored their brothers, and hero-worshipped them openly in a way quite novel to my experience. They were always dashing about, to various stations, to friends, down to Sydney, to race meetings; and flirting with various young men whom they referred to always as 'coupons' – I suppose a relic of the war.

Presently Archie and Belcher arrived, looking jaded by their efforts. We had a cheerful and carefree weekend with several

OVERLEAF: *Ten-month sugar cane in Queensland.*

unusual pastimes, one of which was an expedition in a small-gauge train, of which I was allowed, for a few miles, to drive the engine. There was a party of Australian Labour M.P.s, who had had such a festive luncheon that they were all slightly the worse for drink, and when they took it in turns to drive the engine we were all in mortal danger as it was urged to enormous speeds.

Sadly we said farewell to our friends – or to the greater portion of them, for a quota was going to accompany us to Sydney. We had a brief glimpse of the Blue Mountains, and there again I was entranced by landscape coloured as I have never seen landscape coloured before. In the distance the hills really *were* blue – a cobalt blue, not the kind of grey blue that I associated with hills. They looked as if they had just been put on a piece of drawing-paper, straight from one's paint-box.

Australia had been fairly strenuous for the British Mission. Every day had been taken up with speech-making, dinners, luncheons, receptions, long journeys between different places. I knew all Belcher's speeches by heart by this time. He was good at speech-making, delivering everything with complete spontaneity and enthusiasm as though it had only just come into his head. Archie made quite a good contrast to him by his air of prudence and financial sagacity. Archie, at an early date – in South Africa I think – had been referred to in the newspapers as the Governor of the Bank of England. Nothing he said in contradiction of this was ever printed, so Governor of the Bank of England he remained as far as the press was concerned.

May 1 (Monday)

My darling Mummy

We arrived at Adelaide Saturday morning. As usual, I was
sea sick for the first half of the voyage, but not quite as bad as
last time. Still it took me a good ten days before I could smile
once more. After that I had rather a merry time. There were
several young people on board and we played silly games every
evening or else danced, and the last three nights we had supper
parties with the Captain or one of the other officers and got
to bed about 3 a.m. I loved it (Archie, needless to say, retired
punctually at half past ten, as usual – but fortunately had no
objection to my being gay, even if he wasn't, though marvelling
at my taste). Then we got up a jazz band which took up a good
deal of time and made an appalling noise. Also played balloons
in which game everybody banged others on the head with a
large balloon.

We sat next to the Captain with a very nice man Mr
Stourton, who has done a lot of buying of polo ponies in the
Argentine for the Millers and others. He looked very ill and
grey in the face and has been sent out to Australia to live for
two years. Also a startling looking girl whom we nicknamed the
'Chorus Girl', a Mrs Longworth whose husband is the champion
swimmer of Australia. She was rather amusing, and when at a
fancy dress evening she actually came as a 'very fast chorus girl',

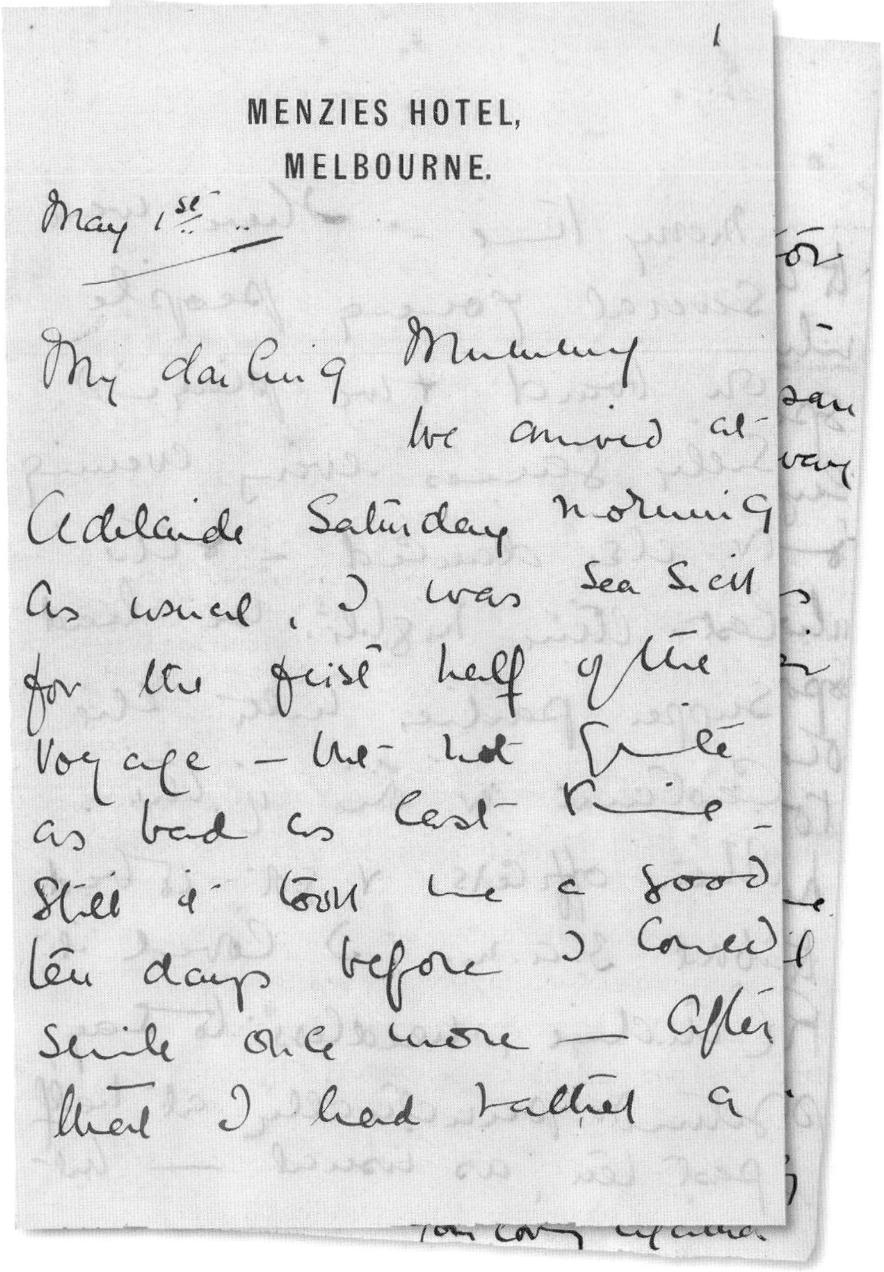

MENZIES HOTEL,
MELBOURNE.

May 1st

My darling Mummy

We arrived at
Adelaide Saturday morning
As usual, I was sea sick
for the first half of the
Voyage — tho not quite
as bad as last time —
Still it took me a good
ten days before I could
smile once more — After
that I had rather a

we could hardly contain ourselves! There was a dear girl called Miss King, a nurse by profession, but perfectly sweet to all the children who adored her. I hope to see her again if we go to Queensland. Mrs Longworth has a jolly little boy of 18 months of whom she takes not the faintest notice. He really is growing up very well in consequence, though it's a marvel he hasn't met his death before this, his mother spending all her time trying dance steps to the gramophone with a fat American commercial

The TSS Aeneas *and Captain Wallace.*

Mrs Tancock

Mrs Mitford

Mr Coleman   Mrs Longworth
Chief Officer   Mr Stor

Archie & Mr Campbell
decide that " Plain ties

traveller! The Captain was an old dear, very bluff and broad, and madly keen on dancing. He and his wife, their children being now launched on the world, have taken up dancing and go to dances together, and are very keen on learning new steps. I was very sorry to leave the Aeneas.

At Adelaide we were met by some representative of the government with the information that Belcher had gone on to Melbourne and was probably in Tasmania by now and we were to follow on, so we left the same afternoon and arrived here yesterday morning. All the people are friendly – and the trains are far more comfortable than in South Africa.

We found Belcher here laid up with a bad leg again and quite tame for the moment! Hiam has gone on to New Zealand. We sail for Tasmania tomorrow. Remain there about a week, get back here and stay about 10 days till the 20th when we may possibly go on a motor tour through the bush to some stations, then to Brisbane and to Queensland, then return to Sydney. Sail the beginning of July for New Zealand.

Today was Labour Day and they came for us in a car and we saw all the processions from the House of Parliament, had a dinner with the President and the Senate, returned here to lunch, afterwards went to the Exhibition Grounds where there were various sports going on, saw Labour enjoying itself, were introduced to all the Labour people who were all very jolly and sporting, including one old gentleman of 106 who told Archie he liked his face. I was introduced to the Champion Lady Runner of Australia and photographed her, and she then failed to win the race!

We went on for a motor tour round the bay. Nothing so far to compare with South Africa in the way of scenery, but it all looks far more prosperous and go ahead – and jollier people.

No letters – I am beginning to despair of ever hearing again from home. But there will be a mail in quite soon. I think.

Lots and lots of love. There was a Baba on the boat just a little smaller than Teddy, but not nearly so attractive. I do want you all so.

Your loving
Agatha

MENZIES HOTEL
MELBOURNE

May 1 [Monday]

Darling Mummy

We saw the Labour Day procession this morning – beautifully decorated wagons and horses, with banners and waving plumes, and '8 hours day' everywhere. We saw it from a window in Parliament House, and afterwards drank ginger ale with the President of the Senate. After lunch, Mr Greenwood of the Industries dept of the Customs whose job it is to take us round, brought a car and his two daughters and ran us out down the St Kilda road (highly praised by Lord Northcliffe) and partly round the bay. On the way, we looked in on the 'Labour Sports', welcomed by Mr Jack Smith, the secretary. The feature of the afternoon was a race between the Champion lady runner of Australia, Mrs Baddock (of who I took a snap shot) the Champion man, and a Champion Goat! The betting was on the goat, but he just finished second to the lady! Archie retired diplomatically to drink with the notabilities of the Labour world, and was told by a veteran of 106 that he lived up to his face, he would be all right! Going round the bay, we were made aware of the importance of the ti tree, a most ordinary looking bush, but apparently the pride of the Australian heart, and they have reserves of it, and absolutely hedge it round with notices 'Anyone damaging shrubs etc.'

Mr Greenwood with Mary and Gladys Greenwood.

On return we fell in with the local Trade Commissioner, furious against Belcher who had not answered his letters and

Mrs Baddock, Champion Runner of Australia at Labour Day Sports.

generally slighted him. A most unpleasant man – but then, to be candid, so is Belcher! Greenwood endeavoured to pacify him, but unavailingly. The matter being mentioned to the Wild Man, he flew into one of his worst rages, and nobody could speak to him for the rest of the day. Enforced teetotalism does not improve his temper!

May 2 [Tuesday]

Wild Man worse than ever this morning. He is in his room darkened like a primeval cave, eating bread and milk, and growling at everybody. I offered to bandage his leg for him, and his polite reply was, 'Why can't I be left alone?' He would not say whether he was going to Tasmania or not, and would not advance any money for anyone else to go. At 2.30, Greenwood and the car were waiting, as the boat sailed at 3 and still nobody dared approach Belcher. But at 2.45 he rushed growling through the hall to the car.

May 3 [Wednesday]

We arrived at Launceston 9.30 this morning after a smooth crossing. Launceston is about 40 miles up the river Tamar which for most of the way is almost exactly like a rather bigger Dart, with the wooded hills sloping down each side. It made me feel quite homesick. Also, it was raining – which was even more reminiscent of England. Two men met us in a cheerful fog as to who or what we were – which did not improve Belcher's temper. We went into the Town Hall and were kept waiting a few minutes while they looked for the Mayor. Fresh explosions from B. When found, he genially asked Belcher who and what he was – I thought he would have apoplexy! We then adjourned to the Commercial Travellers Club for ginger ale and 'squash lemons', Belcher muttering: 'There's only one thing to do I shall go back to Melbourne the first thing tomorrow morning!' Fortunately, he was asked to make a short speech, which slightly restored him, but a further crushing blow awaited him at the station. No saloon – merely a first class reserved carriage! He really does think he is a King, or Lord Northcliffe – it's a sort of – do I mean megalomania? It's increased very much even since South Africa. Hiam only got him by train to Melbourne by getting them to assure him that even Hughes always shared a compartment with his secretary. He missed a very good trip in the West through the bush, by sending word that at any station (settler's house) he must be assured of a room to himself, and that he could not start at 6 in the morning, but that if they would send another car at 8 he would follow on. The man who was taking them (a very influential station holder) completely lost his temper, and said through the telephone to Hiam, who repeated the message verbatim with, I fancy, a good deal of enjoyment, 'that the Major could damned well stop away, he'd taken better men than him who were content to share rooms.' So Bates and Hiam went alone, and had a most interesting trip, and Belcher has been secretly furious ever since, and got Greenwood

to fix him up another trip through the bush down here. Which was done, but the Trade Commissioner who hates Belcher, as I told you, stepped in and made mischief, and the man who was arranging it sent a formal note saying he regretted it couldn't be done, as he might be going away any minute. Australians will *not* stand 'side' – they are extraordinarily nice and kind, and awfully hospitable, but 'swank' does not go down well.

To return to our train to Hobart to begin with I shouldn't think they possessed a saloon, the whole train consists of two coaches of the old fashioned type without corridors, and an antique engine, built in Manchester in 1891 which leaks badly and has several holes in the funnel! A magnificent luncheon basket had been put in, with cold chicken and ham, salad all mixed, a French apple tart, a great pot of thick cream, and new bread and butter. Belcher, instead of sitting in a corner with his leg up, as anyone in his senses would, and as we all suggested, sat in the middle, with his back against an arm, with the air of a complete martyr, and said nothing in the luncheon basket was fit for him to eat. Nobody cared however! We let him sit there and we strained ourselves to our fullest capacity to leave no delicacies behind! Sure enough when we got out at Parattah to stretch our legs, (they wait there for twenty minutes) we peeped in, and there was Belcher devouring bread and butter, and for the rest of the way on, he had a whole half of the carriage to himself!

We arrived at Hobart at 6, and were met by Mr Addison, the Premier's secretary, a pleasant, but rather vague young man, who again did not kow tow sufficiently to the wild man, who retired to his room in high dudgeon. You can't imagine how *farcical* it all is! But at the same time very wearing, and spoils what would otherwise be such a pleasant trip. Archie and I went out and walked round Hobart. It is a *lovely* place – quite cold this time of year, but delicious air, crisp and invigorating. Mountains all round, and very deep blue water. It is five miles up from the mouth of the Derwent but such deep water that big ocean going steamers can come right along side the wharf. It's like a mixture of the Lakes and Devon. I should have liked to have stayed there weeks. The next morning, the Mayoress, Mrs Snowden, sent me an enormous bunch of lovely chrysanthemums. After lunch we went to see over Jones jam factory. Sir Henry Jones himself did not show us over, and that offended Belcher who became sulky once more. And tasted canned fruit, and said it was rotten, and was really most rude. We were to go on to the Exhibition of Tasmanian goods which was on (and which we discovered later had been got up solely for us) but B. said his leg was too bad, so A. and I went – found the Mayoress and everyone waiting to receive us, and were formally conducted round the place and photographed. We explained B's absence as best we could, exaggerating his leg, and calmed everyone down, and Archie made quite a good speech – without mumbling, speaking quite distinctly, and we were welcomed in another speech, and it was quite a public ceremony! On our return to the Hotel, we found B. still further incensed because Addison had sent in our itinerary, and on Saturday afternoon, Archie was put down to attend the races with Sir Elliot Lewis, the Treasurer (and principal official in the absence of the Premier) whereas Belcher was to go off and inspect some Zinc works with a mere subordinate. He did nothing but repeat 'You and Sir Elliot Lewis' and snort.

Friday [May 5]

Started by car at 8.30 this morning for Waddamana, the Electric Power Station. They have a lot of water power from big lakes on the central plateau in Tasmania, and so have very cheap power. At Cadbury's works it is 3/8d in unit – domestically about 1d. The wild man was more or less restored to good humour, having had three reporters to interview him the night before, the prospect of meeting the Premier on his return on Monday, and having conceived the idea that it was necessary for Archie to go to Launceston that night and spend Saturday and Sunday there so as – 'not to offend the North'. This was accepted with all gravity, but we took a sly peep at the amended itinerary and noticed that Major Belcher was now accompanying Sir Elliot Lewis to the Races!

It was a glorious run to Waddamana, up 3000ft, and very cold, but through beautiful country, all silvery blue gums. All Australian scenery that I have seen has a faintly austere quality, the distance is all a soft *blue* green – sometimes almost grey – and the white trunks of the blue gums give a totally different effect, and here and there great clumps of trees have been ringbarked and have died, and then they are ghost trees, all white, with white waving branches. It's all so – virginal – if there

OPPOSITE:
The countryside around
Waddamana.

Mr Moore Robinson (left) and Sir Eliot Lewis.

were nymphs in the woods, they would never be caught.

Major Butters, the Managing Director of the Power Co. and us, and a Col. Hurley, the Commonwealth Emigration Officer, and a man called Moore Robinson, Librarian and Publicity Officer. He was charming, and told me most interesting things about the early history of Tasmania, and the original bushmen (who died out in 1871). They were quite different from the bushmen of the mainland, and were supposed to be the earliest race known, from which we all spring, coming originally from the West of India passing East across Asia and Australia (joined then) and as far south as they could go. Then Tasmania was separated from the mainland. In the mainland they died out quite soon. This is supported by a particular kind of animal (a tiger cat, I think) which is still found in Tasmania, but which in Australia has been found in the fossil state, having died out about twenty thousand years ago. These Tasmanians were neither negroid, nor Polynesian (Maoris), but had straight black hair. Another interesting thing he told me was that the certain peculiarities of the 'Neanderthal' man, in particular the shin bone, and the bicuspid, reappear occasionally in the Maoris of New Zealand at long intervals, and particularly in certain families. We had lunch at Waddamana and saw all over the Power station, which is in a lovely deep gorge. The water comes from the Great Lake, with a fall of 1100ft in pipes down a steep hill. The Power house cat, alas, ignored the notice of 'Danger, live wire' the other day, leapt on a terminal and received a current of 6600 volts. Terrible flash – and absolutely no cat!

We started home about 5.30 talking Neanderthal men for all we were worth and I am going with Mr Moore Robinson to the Museum tomorrow morning, and he will show me round. We got home at 10, and Archie had to dash for the station to catch the night train to Launceston.

Saturday [May 6]

Most interesting visit to the Museum. *The* feature is the Nototherium Mitchelli, a marvellous skeleton of an extinct marsupial rhinoceros which is unique in the world. Nowhere else is such a thing known, and they have been offered untold sums by America for it, but though poor, they have clung to their Nototherium, and steadfastly refused to part with it. There were death casts of several of the Aborigines, and a great collection of sketches and water colour drawings of the Tasmania of 100 years or so ago – some of them perfectly lovely – done on that pale yellow and grey paper and just tinted. Then one of the arrival of the dogs, a row of whom were to be placed on the isthmus of a peninsula to prevent the escape of the convicts at night. Eight or ten of them, bounding out of barrels and being reviewed by the Governor, Sir John Franklin! Also a 'proclamation' issued by him to the natives. A pictorial one since they couldn't read or write. All in colours. At the top arrival of white men in boats, black men peering at them from behind trees. Next line, on the right the Governor in cocked hat with staff behind, shaking the hand of a black chief with wives and children attendant. Next, on the left, black man spearing a white one, on right, black man being hung by Governor. Last, on left, white man killing a black one, on right, white man duly hung in accordance with strict justice. The pictures are awfully quaint, though. I saw more drawings and sketches in the Royal Society's private room. Mr Moore Robinson is also going through all the early records and there is one delightful account in a newspaper of a sale of a wife. 'Mr So and So brought to the hammer his wife Anne. She was knocked down to Mr Blank for the goodly sum of a bottle of rum and twenty ewes. Had the lady been more prepossessing in appearance, doubtless the bidding would have been more brisk!' I like the last candid touch. Also an advert: 'Notice. Whereas my wife has run off with some damned fellow, anyone found harbouring her will be prosecuted with the utmost vigour of the law.' It was a most enjoyable morning. In the afternoon, the Races, with Sir Elliot Lewis and a complacent Belcher. We had tea there with Mrs Lyon, wife of the President of the Racing Club, and sat in the Governor's box (further improvement of B's temper). Came out about square on the day. Mrs Lyon was very jolly. Bridge in the evening at the Ladies Lyceum Club – the funniest Bridge I have ever struck. Only six had collected – so we played two 'threes' under peculiar local rules which included the 'one who was farthest behind not paying because it was such bad luck.' In honour of my presence, the stakes were raised from 1d to 3d. They were all most kind, and had brought me a beautiful bunch of roses. Mrs Snowden, the Mayoress, and a Mrs Mulock (?) represented a more modern element, and were quite interesting to talk to. We were playing together at the end, disregarding local rules and having rather fun. They are going to send to Melbourne for my book.

Sunday [May 7]

Bates and I motored to Launceston. I was sorry to leave Hobart – its such a beautiful place, and there's so much to see all round it that I hadn't time for. It was icily cold motoring. I shall be sending a postcard to Punkie soon with the words CHIL BLAINS on it! Just when she is sweltering in a July sun! Give me the tropics. Launceston as you come into it from the south

MISSIONERS IN TASMANIA.

GREAT DEVELOPMENTAL OUTLOOK.

LAUNCESTON, May 7.

Colonel Christie, of the British Exhibition Mission, arrived at Launceston from Hobart yesterday morning, and in company with Mr. H. K. Fysh (president of the Chamber of Manufactures) and Alderman G. Shields, visited White Hills, Evandale, and Longford. Colonel Christie had been anxious to see the agricultural country, and he was much impressed with the prolific appearance of the districts mentioned. The country, he said, reminded him of the rural portions of England. The visitor spent the afternoon at golf, accompanied by Mr. A. E. Ferrall (president of the Chamber of Commerce), and as the weather was ideal for the links, the trip proved of special interest to Colonel Christie.

Advantage was taken of the fine morning to motor him down the west bank of the Tamar to Exeter, where some of the best orchards of the district are located. Mr. Fysh, Mr. E. Ritchie (Master Warden of the Launceston Marine Board), and Hon. Tasman Shields (Honorary Minister) accompanied the visitor. At Blackwall large quantities of apples, packed and graded for shipment, were seen, and the return run to Launceston was made via Bridgenorth. To-morrow morning, in company with Mr. F. W. Bates, who arrived from Hobart to-night, and Messrs. H. K. Fysh and A. C. Ferrall, a visit will be paid to various factories and other places of interest in and around the city. The visitors will leave by the steamer Nairana for Melbourne in the afternoon.

In conversation with a "Mercury" representative, Colonel Christie said he had been much impressed with the extent of the Great Lake hydro-electric scheme, which he had visited before coming to Launceston. More factories were needed in Tasmania, but an abundance of cheap power would soon make the State widely known as a manufacturing centre. Regarding the North, he thought that more population was needed, but considered that the extension of power would do much to induce more people to settle. He considered the works at Waddamana quite adequate to provide for vast development in the industrial life of Tasmania.

Colonel Belcher, another member of the mission, will come to Launceston on Tuesday morning, and will leave during the day for Burnie, where he will catch the steamer Oonah for Melbourne.

is Newton Abbot to the life! And all the names are so familiar round here. Chudleigh, Exeter etc. – it made me long for home! Found Archie with a bad cold, and very nearly frozen alive with motoring all and every day. The fact that, in Launceston, they never ride less than nine in a car, though productive of discomfort, probably saved his life.

Monday [May 8]

Walked up the Cataract Gorge, which is beautiful. Sides like the rock walk. It continues for two miles up to the inevitable Power station. Bates, A. and I left at 2.30 by the S.S. Nairana for Melbourne. Belcher arrives in Launceston tonight, and is to motor tomorrow through some timber country and a butter and cheese farm to Burnie and take tomorrow's boat from there.

Tuesday, May 9

Back in Melbourne, where it is raining – and anyway one city is much like another. I miss Tasmania. Preparations are going forward for the 'Bush trip' desired by Belcher. I shall enjoy that if there is room for me, but they mayn't want to send two cars and I don't see how we shall all get into one. One great discovery. A parcel which Belcher and Archie having been carrying about under the impression it was cigarettes turns out to be mail! A letter from you and one from Punkie whom I have been reproaching bitterly (but anyway, it's only *one* though I admit a good one!) Awfully exciting about her play! And I shall be furious if she arrives 'on the film' before I do! It seems as though there was such a thing as an agent who is some good. I've been rather idle – but have written a Grand Guignol sketch and a short story.

I think the regular mail only goes every fortnight from here. Another letter came in from you by the boat today. It *is* lovely to hear from you. It will be heavenly when I get back and see you. When Belcher is at his worst, I console myself by the thought that I have had nearly £200 of free railway travel, and one must put up with something for that! I speak to him as little as possible now, am just quietly polite! And sometimes it is really screamingly funny! He does think he is so important, and that

The final of a boat race in Melbourne.

everyone is impressed by him. He ought to go into Parliament (that is what he really is aiming at) because he's a *very* good speaker, and 'publicity' is the breath of life to him, and when he's a Government official, with four of five private secretaries, the more he muddles things, the more in his element he will be!

Love to Mont, and Madge and James and Jack and Joe and Rip AND ROSALIND!

Agatha

Have sent you the 'Herald' with my picture in it! [see page vi]

Menzies Hotel
Melbourne

May 10 [Wednesday]

My darling Mummy

We went yesterday afternoon to see over MacRobertson's chocolate factory. Very interesting. All the sacks of different kinds of cocoa beans, Trinidad, Ceylon, West African, New Guinea, New Hebrides etc. The way you blend these is the great secret and art of chocolate making. They [are] roasted and passed through a machine which sorts husks from kernels, then into one that grinds them, and another that rolls the powder smooth. Some of the beans have the cocoa butter extracted (after which they are used for cocoa) and the extra butter is added to the chocolate. There are machines for stamping and cutting chocolate into cakes and for wrapping it up in waxed paper and outer wrapper. All their things are called 'Old Gold'

May 10

My darling Mummy

We went yesterday afternoon to see over MacRobert-son's choccolate factory. Very interesting. All the sacks of different kinds of cocoa beans, Trinidad, Ceylon, West African, New Guinea, New Hebrides etc. The way you blend these is the great secret and art of chocolate making Then roasted and passed through a machine which sorts husks from kernels, then into one that grinds them, and another that rolls the powder smooth. Some of the beans have the cocoa butter extracted (after which they are used for cocoa) and the extra butter is added to the chocolate. There are machines for stamping and cutting chocolate into cakes and for wraping it up in waxed paper and outer wrapper. All their things are called "Old Gold" and wrapped in that colour. Chocolate creams are amusing, the cream centres pass on a "moving stairway" over a wire mattress arrangement that coats them underneath with chocolate and then under an arch that drips chocolate on their tops and sides and then where two drips make the wiggles on top, and lastly through a refrigerating pipe which dries and hardens them. We also saw boiled sweets and nougat and everything you can imagine in the sweet line. Old MacRobertson came and wrapped in that colour. Chocolate creams are amusing, the cream centres pass on a 'moving stairway' over a wire mattress arrangement that coats them underneath with chocolate and then under an arch that drips chocolate on their tops and sides and then where two drips make the wiggles on top, and lastly through a refrigerating pipe which dries and hardens them.

We also saw boiled sweets and nougat and everything you can imagine in the sweet line. Old MacRobertson came round with us part of the time, tightly buttoned up in white linen, with a kind of Homburg hat with large diamond shaped pieces cut out of it! He started by making sweets in a bathroom in a tumble down house on Monday, Wednesdays and Fridays, and selling them in a tray on his head on Tuesdays, Thursdays and Saturdays, and his factory is built round the old house. We saw stables full of white horses, all called after sweets 'Milk Kisses' and an old Irishman showed us all the decorations, shields etc. that they were in processions and which he designs himself and makes. We ended up in the office where old Mac brought several boxes of chocolates – and our hopes rose – but alas, he merely expatiated on their beauties, and we drove away while he stood with them clasped in his arms smiling us adieu!

Thursday [May 11]

Freda Sternberg, a journalist friend of Mrs Snowden, the Mayoress of Hobart, came and lunched with me. She is going to write some things about the book and me in the Herald, and I am having a photograph taken 'for the Press' tomorrow morning. The wild man returned from Tasmania yesterday afternoon. He dined at the club (to save a shilling, but as he forgot to give up his room on leaving, and they kept it for him, the saving will not be appreciable). A fresh economy has occurred to him (since he is now a teetotaller) that all members of the mission shall pay for their own drinks! We are resisting to the last ditch!

Friday [May 12]

Was photographed for the Herald. Rather like Mr Pecksniff and Salisbury Cathedral, from the North East, from the North West, from the East, from the South, from the South East' etc. Had tea with Freda Sternberg in the Herald office, another quite amusing woman there.

Sunday [May 14]

Went out with Freda Sternberg to a place called Wombalano, Ringwood, about an hour from Melbourne, to spend the day with some friends of hers, the Walkers. She was a well known journalist, and is a most amusing woman. She married a man much younger than herself who does artistic decoration work. Everyone said she was mad, but they have been extremely happy. It was a lovely walk up from the station, through blue

The gardens at Wombalana, Ringwood.

gums, and the hills in the distance actually the colour of Sapphires. About fifteen dogs greeted us and seven or eight Persian cats! She is interested in an industry of bark from the gum trees, dyed and plaited, and made into baskets, mats etc. by blind and crippled soldiers. Flowers look lovely in the baskets, especially low ones like pansies and crocuses etc. I bought some and am sending them home by post – addressed to me at Torquay. Open them if you like – or not it its too much trouble. Mrs Walker has a rather fascinating small niece called Mary,

Mrs Walker and her niece Mary (below) with the dogs.

aged ten who after looking at me a long time remarked 'We've got a dog called Christie.' I said I hoped he was a nice one and Mary responded. 'Yes, but you're not as fair as he is!' Sad – as the dog was a black and tan.

Monday [May 15]

Visited the Sunshine Harvester Works and saw ploughs and all kinds of agricultural machinery being made. Quite interesting.

Thursday [May 18]

Have done some writing of short stories during the last few days. This morning we started at early dawn for Castlemaine accompanied by the Premier of Victoria, Mr Lawson, who is charming. Two compartments were reserved for the party, but Belcher explained he must have one to himself and his secretary as he had to work on the train. However a lot of the Premier's friends and hangers on were on the train and overflowed into Belcher's reserve – so he couldn't work, and had the additional annoyance of knowing that we had the 'best people' in ours. We had great fun, a Mr Thompson, General Manager of the works we were going to see, a most quaint little man and an old friend of Lawson's leading the merriment. 'Civic Reception' at Castlemaine, ginger ale and usual speeches at the Town Hall, on to engineering works and to lunch at the Hotel. All round

Castlemaine was the old gold country, where all the bushrangers were, and the ground all round is turned and looks like a battle ground after bombardment. A cheerful lunch with much discussion of cloth and shoddy and everyone saying 'Well, look at *this* suit! I paid—' etc. After lunch we went over a wool place, and saw blankets being made, and then on to a Pottery place. Then home and I was taken in the evening to an amateur Australian play by one of their 'coming' dramatists whose hand

Mr Thompson and Mr Lawson.

I was taken behind to shake afterwards. Like all plays of the soil, you start with two unprepossessing old men sitting on a bench and exchanging uninteresting remarks with a good deal of 'Oh Aye'! But it was quite interesting.

Tomorrow we start by car at 7.50 a.m. return to dinner with the Governor, and start on Saturday same hour to be away until Wednesday touring various districts, so I shall send this off now.

Lots of love to all. I am awfully excited about Madge's things. I've had another good letter from her, and a good one from James *all* about Rosalind, and Archie is much comforted to think that someone speaks of Daddy to her. I miss her much worse lately.

Your loving Agatha

MENZIES HOTEL
MELBOURNE

Friday [May 19]

Darling Mum

Another start at dawn – this time by car to Warburton to see the wood distilleries there and the timber forests and saw mills. Two of the directors, Mr Russell Grimwade and Mr Stewart, called for us, and Stirling Taylor and MacGregor, the Trade Commissioner, who after furious rows with Belcher is now sweeter than honey – he is a black Scot with high cheek bones and wears a white collar two inches higher than any I have

Warburton: riding on chaff bags (top), Mr Stewart, Agatha and Belcher (middle), and Agatha in a fern gulley (bottom).

Tree ferns.

ever seen. We reached Warburton and from there went on by truck drawn by horses through the bush. Piled up bags of saw dust were arranged for us to sit on. We wound in and out of the trees for about two hours, lovely great straight trees, and great tall umbrella ferns. It was lovely. Arrived finally at Mill No 3 – which is perched on a great mound of sawdust which smoulders away – it has been alight for three years. Nobody has ever found a use for sawdust, a very small quantity is used for packing and for stuffing dolls, but nothing like a quarter of what is wasted. They've tried making briquettes out of it, but it hasn't been a success. We saw a tree felled, and various trees being cut up – mostly poor timber which they were slicing for fruit boxes.

Mr Stewart was a very interesting man – seems to be

a director of every company in the world! He told me that immediately after the war, a secret commission went over to Germany to report on what German women had done during the war. It was never published but he read it. They broke down every where – except in the dressmaking trades, but they had to be sent home from factories, never would handle explosives at all, and were no good on the land, and had to be replaced everywhere by men again.

There was a small state school out there, where the children were learning songs. All the Australian children are nice good manners, and not shy – noisy voices! My Rosy Posy could be the queen of the 'Naows' out here. They sang me Annie Laurie much to the disgust of one small boy who exclaimed: 'That's no good! *I* don't know it!'

We got back rather late, and had a great rush to get to Government House by 7.30 where we were dining. The usual useful A.D.C. greeted us, and explained our positions at dinner, and we were then lined up round the room – I presume in order of precedence, A. and I did not do badly being only beaten by the Archbishop and spouse and an Admiral. Then 'His Excellency the Governor and the Countess of Stradbroke' swept in and shook hands all down the line. We dined at various small tables – and a very good dinner too, better than Cape Town Government House. Lady Stradbroke is quite interesting, tall and dark and haggard, artistic I should think, but distinctly amusing to talk to. The Archbishop broke the ice by inquiring of Belcher whether he had a cousin at Beckenham. B: 'I *had*.' A.B. (delightedly): 'Exactly! Why, my dear fellow, *I* buried him!'

Mr Grove, the Governor's secretary, who sat the other side of me at dinner is a very beautiful young man with an eyeglass, almost exactly like Mr Stewart. I gather he is an extravagant younger son, and was at one time a sergeant in the Police out in Rhodesia! He knew all our friends out there.

Archie took in a Mrs Lyon who remarked at once that she didn't know what to do with her husband. 'He's only thirty five and won't go anywhere.'

After dinner the A.D.C. were very busy, sorting and remixing people. I had a dose of the Archbishop, and a very nice man called Winter-Irving who knows Torquay very well, was there a winter or two ago, and spent all his schooldays there as a boy, and finally a genial man with a completely indistinct voice. He then talked to Belcher, and on comparing notes we were all agreed that he had asked us to something in Sydney, but what and when we still don't know! At 10.15 Mrs Archbishop, instructed by the A.D.Cs, made a move.

Belcher very pleasant. Governors suit him! He expected some high official to come down and conduct him through this Riverina tour we are doing next week through New South Wales. Instead of which a 'mere clerk' from the Tourist bureau!

Saturday [May 20]

7.50 a.m. start this morning! Mr James of the Gippsland Progress something or other came and hustled us off in a fairly small car which already contained a cheerful chauffeur called Arthur, a lady friend of Mr James (unexplained) and a cinema

A house moving to a new site.

operator complete with machine! (Belcher goes on a different tour with Bates). We reached first a place called Dandenong where the President of the Shire (A mayor by any other name etc.) and some local councillors greeted us. Without pausing for the customary ginger ale we dashed to a brick field which Archie inspected, while the cinema operator cinemad him inspecting it! A rival brickfield where one of the workmen was making plaques of Italian deigns of Venus for his own pleasure. A freezing works. A dried milk place. A rapid cup of tea and excellent cake and onwards – as soon as we could pass a house which was being removed bodily from one spot to another (I enclose a photo of it)! On for forty miles to Warrigal, and lunch with another President of the Shire. Then we were transferred

OPPOSITE AND OVERLEAF: *The bush train, including Agatha sitting on the engine (far right).*

into two Ford cars, a Mr Gay joining us who had charge of
the arrangements for the timber forest. Also Arthur appeared
changed into mufti, and prepared to be the life and soul of
the party, exchanging quips freely with his master. Another
thirty miles over appalling bumpy roads and into the heart of
the wooded country right down into the valley where a dozen
wooden shacks represent the budding township of Noojee.
There a 'bush tram' was awaiting us. The usual truck with
wooden boxes to sit on, and what Harry Lauder described as a
'wee pug engine'. I rode part of the way on the engine! (as you
can see in snap shot) It was lovely all through the bush, very
dense undergrowth, and the great tall tree trunks. The engine
flung out showers of sparks, but a kindly stoker was on duty to
extinguish me if I was smouldering in more than two places at
once! We got out at the Goodwood Saw mills, right in the heart
of the forest. I shall never forget it. It was dark when we got back
to Noojee and motored a mile up the valley to the boarding
house where we were to stay the night. Very clean and nice, and
the usual Australian meal, a plate with a slice of beef, a slice of
turkey, a slice of ham, some parsnips, some carrots, two kinds
of potatoes always, bread sauce, horseradish and stuffing and a
portion of Yorkshire pudding, and a good strong cup of black
tea. Then Apple pie and enormous jugs of cream, everyone had
about half a jug each.

To be continued.

Yours

Agatha

Darling Mum

We've been rushing about so that I've forgotten
where I left off in my diary - I think at Gippsland in the
timber forests. The next morning we were got up early and
had breakfast early with theexception of Mr James. Arthur,
the chauffeur, took him his breakfast observing cheerfully
"What I say is, look after a god boss, and he'll look after
you!=" A lovely morning going up another valley in a
bush tram again, and some cinema work : Us passing etc and

then we left regretfully. Fragment of conversation between
James and the democratic Arthur.
A
A. Why did you say we'll be back by 7 ?
J. I promised Col Christie he should sit down to dinner at 7
A. We'll do it by 6 30 and he can have a bath as well.
J. He can't have a bath in half an hour.
A Nonsense, we're not all like you - making a weekend at the
    seaside of it!

Monday.
    Started at 6 45 a.m. by train for Shepperton. Breakfast

at Seymour where the local baker accosted us and accompanied
us on. (Two hours solid talking) Reception by the Shire
and one hour's talking in the Hotel accompanied by ginger ale.

[undated]

Darling Mum

We've been rushing about so that I've forgotten where I left off in my diary – I think at Gippsland in the timber forests. The next morning we were got up early and had breakfast early with the exception of Mr James. Arthur, the chauffeur, took him his breakfast observing cheerfully 'What I say is, look after a good boss, and he'll look after you!' A lovely morning going up another valley in a bush tram again, and some cinema work: Us passing etc and then we left regretfully. Fragment of conversation between James and the democratic Arthur.

A. Why did you say we'll be back by 7?

J. I promised Col. Christie he should sit down to dinner at 7.

A. We'll do it by 6.30 and he can have a bath as well.

J. He can't have a bath in half an hour.

A. Nonsense, we're not all like you – making a weekend at the seaside of it!

Monday [May 22]

Started at 6.45 a.m. by train for Shepperton. Breakfast at Seymour where the local baker accosted us and accompanied

us on. (two hours solid talking) Reception by the Shire and one hour's talking in the Hotel accompanied by ginger ale. Lunch and a 'lady' procured for me (a very nice one, Miss Sutherland, daughter of the solicitor, a dear old Scotchman) and we motored to the canned fruits. If you are buying canned peaches Shepperton Packing Co. Green Label 'Fancy' are good. On to a freezing works, interesting until a certain spot is reached where they render down the offal – when the smell drives you rapidly from the spot! A dinner of thirty that night and I believe Archie spoke quite well. I spent the evening with Miss Sutherland and her sister. Then back to the Hotel and to bed in a bed smelling strongly of stale commercial travellers. (The little Corona has gone wrong, you note!)

Tuesday [May 23]

Saw some citrus fruit on the Returned Soldier's Irrigation Settlement. Does not look as good as South Africa. Then we were motored to the Dookie Agricultural College and had lunch there. And met Mr Pye, a rather celebrated Wheat breeder – quite a genius, delightfully vague, but lyrical on the subject of his crosses. He started experimenting in pre-Mendel days, and about twenty years ago wrote a paper on the subject for an Australian paper which refused it saying 'Who do you think is going to read this stuff?' to which he returned 'I never thought *you* would' send it to an American paper where it appeared, and was subsequently reprinted in pamphlet form and translated into French, German, Russian, Spanish and Italian. The other day the original Australian paper reprinted it! He endeavoured to take a photo of us, but unfortunately let the light in! They offered him treble the salary he is getting to go to South Africa, but he liked his work here and wanted to finish it. For a time he was head of the College but such chaos resulted that other arrangements were speedily made.

A terrible slow journey back to Melbourne in a stopping train, with sausages bolted standing up at Seymour.

Wednesday [May 24]

Went to dine with the Royal Colonial Institute at the Grand Hotel. I sat next to Lord Stradbroke, and found him delightful. Archie was feeling very 'sicky dogs,' thought he could go, but had to bolt in the middle of dinner. Sir James Barrett made quite a good speech, though with inaccurate historical references that tried Belcher sorely (his speciality being history).

Thursday [May 25]

Various odd jobs and frenzied packing by the whole Mission. We got off at last. A strange little man, Mr Cocks, has been sent down by the New South Wales Government to pilot us. He is quite useless, does nothing, and knows nothing. We arrived at Echuca, the border town about 10.30 at night,

Mr Cocks.

and were received at the usual evil smelling Hotel by a drunken ruffian (who apparently acts as chambermaid) and a supercilious young lady. Our room again reeked of stale commercial traveller, and I flung up the window – but the atmosphere grew no better, I discovered why next morning, rows of commercial travellers were sleeping outside on the balcony. The 'Chambermaid' arrived with 'hot water' a tea cup half filled with luke warm water. We descended to breakfast to find that Belcher had 'gone wild' again, was pacing up and down in a hastily improvised sitting room and office saying nobody helped him, that he would make these people understand he must have a clear three hours a day for work, that he should type and dictate all the morning, and would not motor to see anything, and that somebody ought to have told the Mayor he wanted his breakfast at 7 a.m. Bates was ill advised enough to remind him that (a) he had said himself

Belcher with a merino ram at Yanga.

that it was more important to see the 'back' country than to do clerical work, and (b) that he had said to the Mayor that breakfast at 8 would be right and suit him perfectly, whereupon Belcher flew into a real rage and said he couldn't stand being argued with by an incompetent secretary! So we started off without him (which was all for the best) and saw a lock which they are putting on the Murray river – the second of a scheme of 26. A lunch of about 20, the Mayors of Echuca and Momaa (the N.S.W. side of the river) spoke, and Belcher, and then we started motoring to Cobram Station, 40 miles away. Perfectly flat country, empty save for sheep and great wide grass roads. We arrived at Cobram about five and went straight out to see the pure bred Merino rams, wonderful looking creatures. A man called Frank gave us the life history of each. The technique is simple. A. holds the ram by the horns, B. divides the fleece carefully and says '*There*'s wool!' and adds conclusively 'Sixty fours' to which C. cry's ecstatically '*Good* sixty fours!' Then A. says 'Over Frank.' B. 'Ay, over.' The struggling ram is neatly reversed, and B. parts the fleece on its underneath, sticks in a little foot rule and cries – '*There*'s a belly for you!' and C., taking up his next cue murmurs huskily and reverentially '3 inches on the *belly*!' You then take its temperature with the foot rule under the arm, and everyone says together '4 inches and three months yet to go!' Belcher kept his end up well, and said 'Sixty fours' with a good deal of sapience. A lovely clean room at the Station with flowers in it. The manager Graham and his wife were very nice. A good dinner and delicious coffee.

OVERLEAF: *Merino rams at Yanga station.*

Saturday [May 27]

Breakfast at 7.45 and a start for Yanga Station. We saw four kangaroos, an 'old man' red kangaroo, and three small blue fliers. Also, later two meditative emus. The country was rather more wooded than the day before, but still quite flat. It was a run of 120 miles and we got to Yanga about 2 o'clock. There is a magnificent lake there, covered with black swans and wild game and birds of all kinds. Mr Bezley the Manager of the Station

Archie, Mr Bezley, Bob, Mr McKenzie and Tommy Cocks.

who has accompanied us up from Echuca is a Devonshire man, and has a brother living near Tiverton. A man called McKenzie, a big land agent, is also with us, and is known as ''Ectorrrr'. He is most diplomatic, and whenever Belcher starts to lay down the law on farming or sheep, 'Ectorr hastily interposes a funny anecdote. B. is still wild, and really his manners to them all are extremely offensive.

Yanga is lovely – on a peninsula on the lake – roses in the garden, a great mass of bougainvillia and jasmine by the house, and further down by the lake great masses of mandarin and naval orange trees, lemon trees and grapefruit, simply laden with fruit. You can sit out in the sun in a long chair and eat mandarins all day long.

*In the gardens
eating the fruit.*

The lake at Yanga.

Sunday [May 28]

We motored round the lake this morning but otherwise spent an idle day – such a treat after all the rushing lately. Oranges, sunlight and rest.

Monday [May 29]

A white mist this morning and very cold. We set out to see the Cultivation camp, and saw a drill drawn by twelve horses which seemed to excite Belcher very much. He took photographs of it from every angle, oblivious of the fact that owing to the mist they were extremely unlikely to come out. The mist cleared finally and the sun got up and we saw another lake and a mob of 2000 sheep. Back to lunch and then farewell to Yanga, and off by car to Hay (88 miles away) I quickly bagged the front seat where you get least wind. B. rather disgusted, and went in state with the baggage rather than being squashed in behind with Archie and Cocks. After about twenty miles (and forty four gates to open) we found that we had missed the track. A desolate feeling. A wide plain all round you, without a human being or habitation in sight as far as the eye can reach. We turned and twisted hoping all was going well till the fan belt of one car broke. We replaced that. Later, a spring in the other car broke, a serious matter requiring some time for repairs. We had to rip a piece of wire off the fence. On again, twilight approaching fast. A second breakdown – then a third – and on again in pitch darkness not at all certain as to where we were. At last we found ourselves driving into someones back yard, with about a hundred dogs giving tongue. There we were directed on our way, and proceeded cheerfully until the front car took a violent detour to the right. Loud protests from Archie whose countenance was glued to a map by the light of a pocket torch. B. explained how the knowledge of men who know the country like our drivers was vastly superior to amateur map readers and A. shut up unconvinced, merely remarking that by the stars we were now going S.W. instead of N.E! We proceeded about five miles and ran into a deserted sheep shearing place with nothing but cart marks leading out of it. Triumph of the Star steering party, and a demand by them that we should retrace

Mr Bartez,
a pineapple farmer, and his
farm (below).

A pineapple plantation.

our steps to where we had turned off. The chauffeurs remained
entirely independent only condescending to address each other
and absorbed in the joy of tracking other motor tracks quite
oblivious of what direction they took. Eventually we got to
Hay, Archie beside himself with hunger, but Belcher, true to
type, storming about demanding an important telegram from
the Prime Minister which ought to have been waiting for him.
Cocks, also true to type, did nothing whatever. Belcher calls
him 'your pal, Tommy Cook' with ineffable scorn.

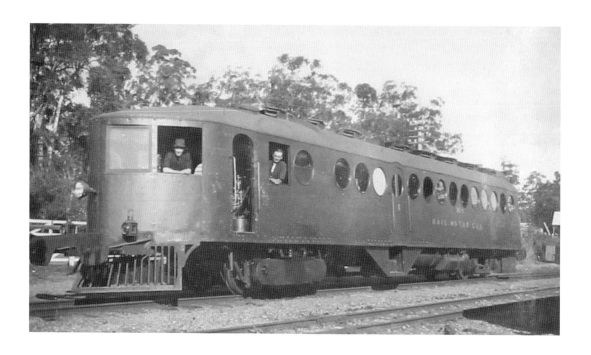

The McKeen Autocar.

Wednesday [May 31]

An early start again. We broke the journey at Yanga and went to see the Irrigation Settlement there in the Murrumbidgee Area. Spent the night at a Government Hydro and on to Sydney.

We arrived here this morning and leave this evening for sunny Queensland. It will be really hot there!

Lots of letters come now from you all. It is lovely.

Yours

Agatha

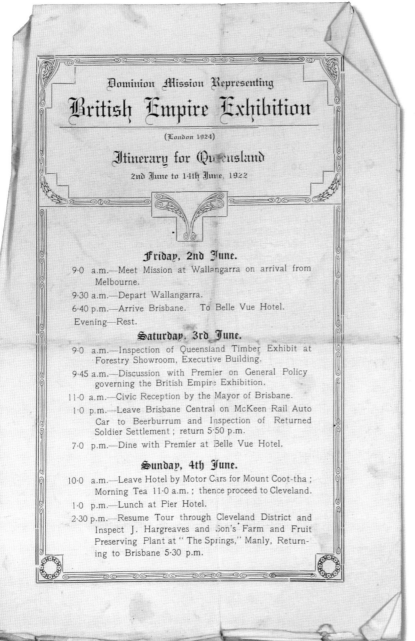

Dominion Mission Representing

British Empire Exhibition

(London 1924)

Itinerary for Queensland

2nd June to 14th June, 1922

Friday, 2nd June.

9·0 a.m.—Meet Mission at Wallangarra on arrival from Melbourne.

9·30 a.m.—Depart Wallangarra.

6·40 p.m.—Arrive Brisbane.   To Belle Vue Hotel.

Evening—Rest.

Saturday, 3rd June.

9·0 a.m.—Inspection of Queensland Timber Exhibit at Forestry Showroom, Executive Building.

9·45 a.m.—Discussion with Premier on General Policy governing the British Empire Exhibition.

11·0 a.m.—Civic Reception by the Mayor of Brisbane.

1·0 p.m.—Leave Brisbane Central on McKeen Rail Auto Car to Beerburrum and Inspection of Returned Soldier Settlement ; return 5·50 p.m.

7·0 p.m.—Dine with Premier at Belle Vue Hotel.

Sunday, 4th June.

10·0 a.m.—Leave Hotel by Motor Cars for Mount Coot-tha ; Morning Tea 11·0 a.m. ; thence proceed to Cleveland.

1·0 p.m.—Lunch at Pier Hotel.

2·30 p.m.—Resume Tour through Cleveland District and Inspect J. Hargreaves and Son's Farm and Fruit Preserving Plant at " The Springs," Manly, Returning to Brisbane 5·30 p.m.

June 23 [Friday]

Dearest Mont.

Many happy returns of today. To get them right I ought to have started six weeks ago! I suppose, absurd as it seems, its almost time to write to Rosalind for *her* birthday. Three candles and I shan't be there!

There's really not much more news to tell you than when I last wrote. We went out to the Blue Mountains for one night. Belcher was too great to go by train – with great persistence he cadged a car – or rather two cars – so we started in style, much to Archie's annoyance. He hates motoring in the cold, and much prefers going by train any day. Our car went well until we started climbing miles from anywhere when it proceeded to turn nasty. We induced it to go on for a bit but it broke down about six times and eventually we arrived at the Jenolan Caves at 6 p.m. instead of 2.30, freezingly cold and dead tired.

After a meal we were taken as a 'special party' (guests of the Government!) round the Orient Cave which is supposed to be the best. It really is wonderful, you go for two miles through the bowels of the earth, up and down steps (1500 in all – and you know it next morning!) twisting in and out through labyrinths and coming to the different chambers, the Egyptian, Indian etc. one with crimson stalactites hanging and great pillars and fringed hanging shawls, and the Indian one is all white. You go along a wire netted path – the first cave they discovered was entirely destroyed in three months by everyone pulling bits off it – and they're not taking any chances now! It's lighted up with electric lights all concealed behind the rocks – really wonderfully done. It takes a good two hours to go round it. The worst thing to bear is the guide's humorous remarks! We were up early the next morning and did some of the open air caves. The Hotel (or Cave House as it is called) is right in the heart of the mountains they rise up all round it, and to get to it the road zig zags down and seems to end, but really it is a great natural arch through the mountain itself. We saw another cave, the, 'Right Imperial' quite different in style, full of very delicate stalactites and miniature fairy grottos you had to lie down on your tummy to see. We had to start back at 2 o'clock unfortunately. I could have spent a week there quite happily.

Tonight Belcher has been dining with some of the Labour Party. To one to them during dinner he recounted one of his famous 'lion' stories, the one I've probably written before about, the man who, rather fuddled, wondered why his team of mules was going at such a splendid pace, and discovered when day broke that he had inspanned two lions as the wheelers! Belcher has told this story many times, sometimes it gets a hearty laugh, sometimes a feeble one, but this time the man merely stared with horror in his eyes and demanded in a hoarse whisper: 'Good God, who un'arnessed em?'

Lots of love, Mont dear, and go on getting better and better. Hope Shebani is well and giving the Sandfords a new interest in life. Look after Mother, and see she changes her clothes after she's been hosing the garden. She's always sopped through.

Your loving

Agatha

Carlotta
Arch

A C Bus

Mr Beal Jun

Devil's
Coachhouse

Carlotta Arch

Caves House

Mr Beal
& Ladys.

My darling Mummy

Woke up on the Friday morning en route to Brisbane
to find we were three hours behind time. We arrived at Wallangarra
and were met by "the honourable the Minister" for Lands, the
Speaker and Mr Troedson of the inevitable Tourist Bureau. We
had a hurried meal (breakfast, because it is the breakfast station
although it was actually lunch time) and then entered the
Queensland train - a special saloon having been attached (Belcher
brightened visibly nd murmured that Queensland seemed to know
how to do things) a retiring cabin luxuriously fitted was placed
at my disposal, and a kindly special conductor put his head in
at intervals to say "Sure you're all right, Mrs Christie? How
about another pillow now?" At various stations we alighted for
Civic receptions. Tea on board, and ginger ale (and whiskey) at
intervals of half an hour. We got into Brisbane about ten o'clock
rather weary.

It was lovely to wake up on Saturday morning to brilliant
sunshine and hot weather again, and red poinsettias and palm trees
growing against the white buildings. Wandered around Brisbane
in the morning and at one o'clock started off by the McKeen Auto
Car with various Ministers and a large crowd of their hangers on

[undated]

My darling Mummy

Woke up on the Friday morning en route to Brisbane to find we were three hours behind time. We arrived at Wallangarra and were met by 'the honourable the Minister' for Lands, the Speaker and Mr Troedson of the inevitable Tourist Bureau. We had a hurried meal (breakfast, because it is the breakfast station although it was actually lunch time) and then entered the Queensland train – a special saloon having been attached (Belcher brightened visibly and murmured that Queensland seemed to know how to do things) a retiring cabin luxuriously fitted was placed at my disposal, and a kindly special conductor put his head in at intervals to say '*Sure* you're all right, Mrs Christie? How about another pillow now?' At various stations we alighted for Civic receptions. Tea on board, and ginger ale (and whiskey) at intervals of half an hour. We got into Brisbane about ten o'clock rather weary.

It was lovely to wake up on Saturday morning to brilliant sunshine and hot weather again, and red poinsettias and palm trees growing against the white buildings. Wandered around Brisbane in the morning and at one o'clock started off by the McKeen Autocar with various Ministers and a large crowd of their hangers on who always come on these trips and pocket cigars and toss down free drinks. We were visiting the Soldier

Bananas at Cleveland.

Settlement at Beerburrum where they grow pineapples and bananas, and where I corrected my original impression that pineapples grew high up on trees instead of about three inches from the ground. I enclose some photos of pines etc. and one of the houses. All the Queensland houses are built high up on four wooden legs as though they were on stilts. You keep turkeys and chickens and general repairs and carpentering underneath. We saw over several farms and ran on into Beerburrum itself where the faithful Autocar was waiting (and incidentally holding up the Northern express from Rockhampton). A box with twelve large pineapples accompanied us! We leapt home at an alarming speed on the 3ft 6 gauge. Glasses crashed off the table right and left. We discovered afterwards that Archie was chatting genially with the engine driver, who, anxious to show off his pet, was 'showing how easily she would do 70'.

The mission proper dined with Ministers, and I dined with Troedson and a General and Mrs Spencer Brown – charming old fashion people. He was in the Boer War and this one too – and was awfully struck by the fine physique of our soldiers as opposed to the Australians! Quite the opposite to what we think, isn't it? But certainly, on the whole, they are *not* big men, rather under medium height, but sturdy looking.

Next morning we drove out by car to Mount Coot – that's where you get a wonderful view over the city of Brisbane – really very beautiful. Then on to lunch at Cleveland with Troedson, a great fat man, member for Brisbane, Kurwan (rather like Ward!) and the member for Cleveland, Mr Barnes. Belcher was asked not to swear or drink, as he was very rabid on both points! Lunch at the Pier Hotel, and then inspection of fruit farms – mostly citrus again, also pines, bananas, mangoes, paw paws, and great fields of arrowroot with red flowers.

Mr Kurwan, MLA, Mr Barnes and Mr Troedson in Cleveland.

Cotton picking, the Australian Cotton Growing Association Building (below), and the youngest cotton picker (left).

Back to the Hotel. Tea on Sunday instead of dinner – boiled eggs, cold ham etc. a meal which always arouses Belcher's temper. He sat in stormy silence for ten minutes and finally delivered himself of all his grievances:

(a) why should he be asked not to swear? He wasn't in the habit of interlarding his conversation with oaths.

(b) *We* had gone in a comfortable car – he had gone in a blinking Ford!

Interruption by Archie: 'It wasn't a Ford.'

B. 'It was. The kind you never change gear, just press harder with your foot, and can't hear yourself speak except when you're going down hill. That's a Ford.'

(c) On the preceding day at Beerburrum, again we had gone in a comfortable car, and he in a Ford.

A. 'They were both Fords!'

(d) Bates had had the whole day off (e.g. from 2.30 p.m.) to go and see an Aunt, and had not had the decency to be back by 5.30. That he had aunts in every city in the Dominions, and that he chose the most inconvenient days to visit them.

(e) That since Bates was so inconsiderate, they would have to sit up until midnight to get through the work, and even then would probably have to cut the whole of tomorrow's programme.

(f) That he liked a decent dinner after a hard day's work – not this filthy meal at the unearthly hour of six.

Having worked off steam, he became better tempered and gave us quite a funny imitation of Mr Barnes' conversational manner. Bates was discovered waiting in the lounge ready for work, and Belcher later cursing him volubly and anathematising all his aunts, decided to do no work at all, and went off to the club to see the English papers!

On Monday I went to the Races with Mrs Theodore, the Premier's wife. She is quite nice – very worn out with children and no servants, and the duties of a Premier's wife on top of it all. All the Mission has been very much impressed by Theodore – Labour or no Labour – as a very able man.

The Mission had departed at 7 a.m. to spend a long weary day in Ipswich, civic reception, factory inspections, lunches and dinners with speeches etc. I dined alone, and a Major Bell whom Belcher and Archie had been confabbing with on cattle the night before, came up and spoke to me, and said his sister was in the Hotel and would like to meet me. They were both awfully nice. 'One of us' as the Lucys say. The first people I have met

The Bell family's cattle station at Coochin Coochin, Queensland.

out here who were! The Prince went out to stay at their station, Coochin, for a few days, and refused to go on to the next place!

The Bells are real Australians, their grandfather came out as a soldier guarding convicts etc. and settled out here. They asked me to come out and stay – Belcher was coming anyway for the weekend and to see cattle. I decided straight away to cut Rockhampton and go, and went up with the girl next day by the evening train, after a somewhat dreary Garden Party at Government House.

It was a long deadly journey of about six hours in a train that crawled. We arrived about ten o'clock after motoring five miles, and the room seemed full of tall energetic girls cooking scrambled eggs over the fire and all talking at once! I went to bed dazed. Lady Stradbroke had wired them that we were coming to Brisbane and that we were all very nice! I was to stay two days, but I stayed a week – from Tuesday to Tuesday. Belcher came on the Sunday and left Tuesday morning. It was a pity Archie couldn't have been there. He would have enjoyed it, instead of having a really terrific programme in Rockhampton and Maryborough to carry out. I sorted out the Bells at last! Mrs Bell is delightful, full of character, and intent on her garden. All her children adore her – and adore each other – very like the Lucy's. They seem to own most of the cattle in Australia, and are really rather like a Royal family with a little country of their own, and look after all their people with great seriousness. Quite the old feudal spirit. Two sons, Ernest and Frick are married and they and their families live on the estate, one a mile away, and the other three miles. Then there is Una (who brought me

OPPOSITE: *The Bell women: Doll, Mrs Bell, Aileen, and Una (bottom).*

Miss Collins and Aileen
on their horses.
'After lunch' (below).

from Brisbane), Doll and Aileen and the two boys, both Majors
in the Flying Corps. They are all mad on horses, and the girls go
about all day in shirts and breeches. It's a pity that side saddles
are unknown out here from my point of view – but I suppose I
should only have got very stiff! They were getting up a show for
their small village on the Friday night, and we made costumes
and rehearsed etc. Doll and I did imitations of Moving Pictures
and 'Film Dramas' and really had the greatest fun, and I sang
and had a great success – possibly owing to Aileen and Victor

who went round the village in the morning carefully creating
the impression that I was Melba's latest pupil and discovery!
They were all over in England during the war. The boys were
training at Beverly and they had a house there – so of course we
knew all the same people. A girl called Margaret Allen and her
cousin Dundas Allen were there also. They live near Sydney but
she has been out in India a lot. Also a Mr Foa, an Englishman
(rather the lardida type who has been in a Hussar regiment)
who is out looking for a job (good pay and mostly supervising!)
and who *would* lay down the law as to how to school horses!
He brought a patent saddle with him which filled their head
stockman with disgust. It was all very funny, 'Ferdinand', as we
called him, in his immaculate clothes, lecturing on horseflesh to

*Ferdinand in his smart
riding gear and Susan
dressed for work in the
garden at Coochin.*

Picnic.

a slightly ribald audience. He was really quite a dear – but one can't see him prospering in Australia. Nobody wants anyone to 'supervise', they want sheer hard manual labour!

I'll send you some snap shots next time of the Bell family and Coochin Coochin. I don't wonder the Prince wouldn't leave. There are three or four Aborigines living on the station. One of them an elderly woman called Susan. She sings queer chants for you and can imitate anyone's walk, but she will never imitate Mrs Bell. 'Mrs Bell good to me. I too much respect Mrs Bell to imitate her.' Her father was the 'King' of the district in his day – King Billy, and when the Prince came she was most anxious to meet him. 'He like me – our fathers both Kings.' He was awfully sweet to her, they said, and they loved him for being so nice to their mother. He was very worried because he was afraid he had turned her out of her room (which he had) and was always anxious to be 'as little trouble to your mother as possible'. His visit has not ended in unmixed pleasure, as ever since then they have had the most abominable series of anonymous letters not from one source only but from half a dozen. I believe the jealousies and heart burnings created everywhere in Australia have been awful – bound to be so, I suppose.

I felt quite one of the family by the time I left! And quite sad to leave. We left Brisbane the next day and sail for New Zealand on the 29th [Thurs]. Archie has an awful cold and is very done up. I went to supper with the Allen's on Sunday night and a Mrs Dangar was there who turned out to be a niece in law of Grannie's friends. There are masses of large white houses all round the harbour.

Lots of love

Agatha

Farewells.

PACIFIC

OCEAN

Cape Farewell

Takaka

Karamea Apple

Karamea Bight

Westport

Motup

Cape Foulwind

NELSON

Brighton

Reefton

Greymouth

Hokitika

SOUTH

Culverd

Waikari

Clifton

Rangiora

Alps

Sheffield

Raleigh

WESTLAND

CANTERBURY

ISLAND

Haast

South Bridge

Southern

Canterb
Bight

Fairlie

Washdyke

Omarama

Waitak

Milford Sd.

Wanaka
L:

Studholme
R.

Kinloch

Albert Town

Kurow

Pukeuri

Queenstown

Ophir

Hampden

CRETARY I.

OTAGO

Hyde

Palmerston

Te Anau

Kingston

Blueskin

Ettrick

OLUTE

Lumsden

NEW ZEALAND

From Australia we went to Tasmania, driving from Launceston to Hobart. Incredibly beautiful Hobart, with its deep blue sea and harbour, and its flowers, trees and shrubs. I planned to come back and live there one day.

From Hobart we went to New Zealand. I remember that journey well, for we fell into the clutches of a man known to us all as 'The Dehydrator'. It was in the days when the idea of dehydrating food was all the rage. This man never looked at anything in the food line without thinking how he could dehydrate it, and at every single meal platefuls were sent over from his table to ours, begging us to sample them. We were given dehydrated carrots, plums, everything – all, without exception, tasted of nothing.

'If I have to pretend to eat any more of his dehydrated foods,' said Belcher, 'I shall go mad.' But as the Dehydrator was rich and powerful, and could prove of great benefit to the British Empire Exhibition, Belcher had to control his feelings and continue to toy with dehydrated carrots and potatoes.

By now the first amenities of travelling together had worn off. Belcher was no longer our friend who had seemed a

PREVIOUS PAGE:
*'The members of the British
Trade Mission on board the
steamer Manuka about to
go ashore in Wellington.
Major Belcher, Mr F W
Bates, Colonel A Christie
and Mrs Christie.'
(The men on either
end are not named.)*

pleasant dinner companion. He was rude, overbearing, bullying, inconsiderate, and mean in curiously small matters. For instance, he was always sending me out to buy him white cotton socks or other necessities of underwear, and never by any chance did he pay me back for what I bought.

If anything put him in a bad temper he was so impossible that one loathed him with a virulent hatred. He behaved exactly like a spoilt and naughty child. The disarming thing was that when he recovered his temper he could display so much *bonhomie* and charm that somehow we forgot our teeth-grinding and found ourselves back on the pleasantest terms. When he was going to be in a bad temper one always knew, because he began to swell up slowly and go red in the face like a turkey cock. Then, sooner or later, he would lash out at everybody. When he was in a good humour he told lion stories, of which he had a large stock.

I still think New Zealand the most beautiful country I have ever seen. Its scenery is extraordinary. We were in Wellington on a perfect day; something which, I gathered from its inhabitants, seldom happened. We went to Nelson and then down the South Island, through the Buller Gorge and the Kawarau Gorge. Everywhere the beauty of the countryside was astonishing. I vowed then that I would come back one day, in the spring – their spring, I mean, not ours – and see the *rata* in flower: all golden and red. I have never done so. For most of my life New Zealand has been so far away. Now, with the coming of air travel, it is only two or three days' journey, but my travelling days are over.

Midland Hotel

Wellington

N.Z.

July 4th

Darling Mummy

A fairly good passage across to New Zealand on the Manuka.
First two days fairly smooth - third day nasty. I lay down
most of it and escaped being sick. I have never seen anything
in my life as beautiful as Wellington harbour. Sydney is nothing
to it. Great mountains all round coming down to the water's
edge - the far off ones with snow on them. Blue sky and deep blue
water and Wellington itself nestling on the side of the mountain.
Mr Dalton, the Trade Comissioner, came on board to greet us with
various other people. He is rather an amusing man, much nicer
than the usual run.

This is an excellent Hotel, lovely food, comfortable beds and
maginificent baths. I found a wire from Mrs Fordham, welcoming
me to N.Z. saying she was sorry she wouldn't see me, but that her
sister would come and call upon m e in Christchurch.

This afternoon, Mrs Collins, wife of our "local Greenwood"
took me round the town, up in a funicular to where you get a wonder
ful view across the bay, looking down on the city and then we
walked down through the Botanical Gardens which are mostly the
untouched bush. She and her husband dined with us, and afterwards
we went to the new Parliament House where a gentleman was making
a speech boasting about "borrowing at par" which aroused Archie's
financial contrmpt.

Wednesday.

Played golf this afternoon with Mrs Collins who is about my
class. Quite an even match, she just beat me. In the evening
I went to Bridge with Mrs Dalton, whilst the Mission dined with
Jellicoe. Rather sad, the secretary wrote that as Lady J was away
no ladies were being invited, and he's the only G.G. I really
wanted to meet! Both B. and A. liked him immensely. I had some
very good Bridge, a Miss Harcourt, and a lady whose name sounded

July 4 [Tuesday]

Darling Mummy

A fairly good passage across to New Zealand on the *Manuka*. First two days fairly smooth – third day nasty. I lay down most of it and escaped being sick. I have never seen anything in my life as beautiful as Wellington harbour. Sydney is nothing to it. Great mountains all round coming down to the water's edge – the far off ones with snow on them. Blue sky and deep blue water and Wellington itself nestling on the side of the mountain. Mr Dalton, the Trade Commissioner, came on board to greet us with various other people. He is rather an amusing man, much nicer than the usual run.

This is an excellent Hotel, lovely food, comfortable beds and magnificent baths. I found a wire from Mrs Fordham, welcoming me to N.Z. saying she was sorry she wouldn't see me, but that her sister would come and call upon me in Christchurch.

This afternoon, Mrs Collins, wife of our 'local Greenwood' took me round the town, up in a funicular to where you get a wonderful view across the bay, looking down on the city and then we walked down through the Botanical Gardens which are mostly the untouched bush. She and her husband dined with us, and afterwards we went to the new Parliament House where gentleman was making a speech boasting about 'borrowing at par' which aroused Archie's financial contempt.

Wednesday [July 5]

Played golf this afternoon with Mrs Collins who is about my class. Quite an even match, she just beat me. In the evening I went to Bridge with Mrs Dalton, whilst the Mission dined with Jellicoe. Rather sad, the secretary wrote that as Lady J was away no ladies were being invited, and he's the only G.G. I *really* wanted to meet! Both B. and A. liked him immensely. I had some very good Bridge, a Miss Harcourt, and a lady whose name sounded like Mrs Bonnica were there and were all charming. The New Zealand people really *are* like English people. Miss Harcourt was particularly charming, and I really spent a delightful evening.

Archie called for me on his way back from Government House and we found on returning that Belcher (who has been

Mr Jellicoe and family (above) at Government House.

in the best of humours lately) had filled our two beds with golf sticks etc. surmounted with hats, A.'s effigy was reading 'The Australian Year Book' and mine 'No Clue!' Jellicoe had told them a story of Smuts – during the war there was a meeting of Premiers to discuss how to preserve the safety of the Empire after the war, Hughes started off with a long speech on every conceivable subject tariffs, White Australia etc. Massey followed with a still longer one. Then Smuts rose and said, 'Mr Prime Minister, in my opinion the safety of the Empire depends entirely on sea communications' and sat down again. Of course both Massey and Hughes dislike Smuts and say he is a pure Revolutionary. I think he is a fine little man.

Thursday [July 6]

We visited a woollen factory this afternoon. B. has long angled for a rug to be presented to him – but so far with no success. He did his best this afternoon – but, alas! for his manoeuvres, they *did* present a rug – a beauty, similar to that given to the Prince and called the 'Prince's Rug' ever since – but they gave it to *me*!

At 7.30 we boarded the tiny steamer – cargo steamer – which was to take us across to Nelson on the South Island. A. and I had the only cabin, B., Bates and Mr O'Brien (who accompanies us in the role of Tommy Cocks) had berths in the dining saloon. It can be the roughest passage in the world going through Cook's Straits, but as it turned out, it was a beautifully smooth passage. We came into Nelson at 8.30 in the morning. Again snow covered mountains all round the bay. Really *beautiful* – far the most beautiful country I have been to. It must be gorgeous in summer. At present, of course, it is all hard frost, though golden sunshine.

It is definitely decided now that A. and I take a fortnight's holiday from the Mission – at Honolulu! Isn't it lovely? The one thing I have always wanted and never thought there was any possibility of my doing. B. will stay on here, and we shall meet at Vancouver.

Rather rushed to catch the mail which goes earlier than I thought. I get lots of letters from you and Madge and it is lovely. Lots and lots of love.

Yours

Agatha

July 7 [Friday]

Darling Mummy

This morning we visited the Cawthron Institute where we had a most interesting time. Professor Easterfield showed us the various soil experiments they are making – trying it with different types of manures, superphosphate, lime etc. and what gives the best results. Then we saw Dr Tilyard the entomologist, who is working on woolly aphis which is ruining the orchards of N.Z. He is making cultures of the tiny wasp, the aphilinus,

Mr Davis, Dr Curtis, Dr Tilyard and Professor Easterfield at the Cawthron Institute.

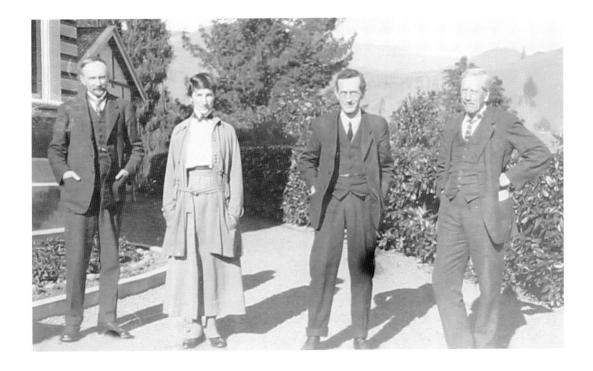

Commercial Hotel

Nelson, N.Z.

July 7th

Darling Mummy

This morning we visited the Cawthron Institute where we
had a most interesting time. Professor Easterfield showed us the
various soil experiments they are making - trying it with different
types of manures, superphosphate, lime etc and what gives the
best results. Then we saw Dr Tilyard the entomologist, who is
working on wolly aphis which is ruining the orchards of N.Z.
He is making cultures of the tiny wasp, the aphilinus, which
makes its home in the body of the aphis and finally eats it up.
They released 200 of them last year. His principle is that every
pest has its own "control" but in a new country one goes without
the other and gets ahead, and then you have to find its control
and introduce it also. Dr Kathleen Curtis, whom we saw next,
does all the vegetable fungus pests such as black spot etc. and
is working on breeding the varieties of apples that are most
immune and finding out why.

A chamber of Commerce luncheon at the Hotel, with the "loyal
toast" and a few brief speeches afterwards. Mr Gilbert (President)
"Gentlemen, charge your glasses" Loud remarks from his political
opponents of "What with?" Mr Gilbert (impervious to the hint)
"Water or tea, anything will do."

Saturday.

Drove out in a big omnibus car, that takes four in each
seat. Belcher did not go. We were quite comfortable to start
with, but picked up anybody of local importance we happened to
meet on the road until the whole car was jammed like sardines.

which makes its home in the body of the aphis and finally eats it up. They released 200 of them last year. His principle is that every pest has its own 'control' but in a new country one goes without the other and gets ahead, and then you have to find its control and introduce it also. Dr Kathleen Curtis, whom we saw next, does all the vegetable fungus pests such as black spot etc. and is working on breeding the varieties of apples that are most immune and finding out why.

A chamber of Commerce luncheon at the Hotel, with the 'loyal toast' and a few brief speeches afterwards. Mr Gilbert (President): 'Gentlemen, charge your glasses.' Loud remarks from his political opponents of 'What with?' Mr Gilbert (impervious to the hint): 'Water or tea, anything will do.'

Saturday [July 8]

Drove out in a big omnibus car, that takes four in each seat. Belcher did not go. We were quite comfortable to start with, but picked up anybody of local importance we happened to meet on the road until the whole car was jammed like sardines. The old jest of 'It is unlucky to ride thirteen in a car' would apply quite seriously to the ordinary New Zealand four seater. They have a passion for loading up. We went up over the Dovedale hills and on to a place called Motueka. It was a long day, but very very lovely, with great snow mountain peaks all round. Very cold, but fine. After lunch, a Mr Isaac Monnoy (with a nose to match his name) showed us some nuggets which excited Bates frightfully (nuggets always do!) and Mr Monnoy was so charmed with his appreciation that they disappeared together and could not be found when we wanted to start and everyone said 'Oh! they've gone to the nail room,' and laughed, and presently they reappeared, breathing port onto the frosty air.

Sunday [July 9]

Mr Gilbert arranged for me to lunch with a Capt. and Mrs Moncrieff who have recently come out from England – charming people with a houseful of the most beautiful things, including some lovely black lacquer and some blue table glass. They have two small boys, and love New Zealand. He has a library of the most interesting new scientific books. I went on to tea with Dr and Mrs Tilyard, and their four small daughters, Patience, Faith, Hope, and Honor. She was a senior wrangler or something and is a most delightful woman. A thoroughly enjoyable day. Belcher and A. played golf.

Monday [July 10]

Great start of the Mission by car down the Buller Gorge to Westport. It is supposed to be one of the most beautiful runs in N.Z. but unfortunately it poured with rain and there was a thick mist over all the mountains, but one could see how lovely it would have been. At about 4 p.m., when we were soaked

Hawks Crag, Buller Gorge.

through and cold beyond belief, a car full of the Westport Progress League arrived to meet us, all very hearty and saying this was typical West Coast weather, and they forced us to get out and visit a funny little coal mine (worked by two brothers!) at the side of the road. B. was not pleased. He said that the only thing that had not been wet were his feet, and now they were wet too. We slid about on wet coal, and saw nothing at all, but got very black. A great race for hot baths at Westport, Belcher and I took all there was, I fear.

Tuesday [July 11]

Pouring with rain again, but A. and I were taken up to
Denniston 2000 feet up on the mountain side to see the coal
mines there. The Manager's wife came up to entertain me, and
we sat by a fire talking solidly for four hours – most tiring to
both of us, while Archie resumed his pastime of sliding about
underground 'and there's nothing to see except coal, and more
coal, and more coal. Saw some of the machinery etc. after lunch
and then back. Mrs Brown came in our car 'if there was room'
as she said. There wasn't, but we increased the number of men
who were sitting on top of each other on the floor from three to
four and managed it quite satisfactorily.

Crossing Buller Gorge.

*Archie in Greymouth
(left) and Bates looking
for nuggets.*

Belcher with camera.

Wednesday [July 12]

Another start in wind and rain for Greymouth – up the
Buller Gorge again which we saw rather better this time, and
it is lovely, a narrow gorge winding in and out amongst the
mountains, with the most wonderful 'bush' tree ferns etc. We
motored to Reefton where we picked up an obsolete train which
went very slowly and landed us at Greymouth in time for dinner
– or rather the inevitable 'tea'.

Thursday [July 13]

A really lovely day – brilliant sunshine. They came for us with
three cars, and three ladies for me, and we went off for a regular
day's joyride, all along the coast to Punakaki, precipice on
the left and the usual narrow road – poor Belcher sits, his fat
shaking like a jelly – he really is nervous motoring! There are
wonderful Nikau palms growing everywhere, and our Torquay
palms which are called cabbage trees, and great tall tree ferns –
it looks far more like tropical scenery than South Africa. There
are some wonderful rocks and 'blow holes' at Punakiki. We had
tea with a Mrs Olney, who was in Torquay during the war, a nice
little woman, sounds Irish. On the way back we stopped at the
'blow up', where they get gold, by pumping water and sand over
wooden tables. I spent the evening with one of my ladies, Mrs
Kitchingham, whilst the Mission had their meeting.

Friday [July 14]

On by car to Hokitika with the most lovely view of the Southern Alps and Mount Cook in the distance – really *beautiful*. Hokitika was an old gold mining town and at one time had thirty thousand people. The beach is *awful* – you look out to sea and then turn round – all the backs of houses and everybody's rubbish is dumped on the sand. In the afternoon we went to see a gold dredger at work and then on to Lake Kaniere. A funny old lady like a dilapidated hen (whom Belcher insisted on calling Mother Seigel) arrived for me – and took an immediate fancy to Archie. She said: 'We'll go in the second car, it's the best. And we'll have your husband.' And when Archie sat in front she said, 'There, I picked you out of all the lot, and you go and sit in front!' Lake Kanieri again is one of the most beautiful

A gold dredger at Hokitiki.

places I have ever seen – mountains all round it and the dense bush down to the water's edge.

The sitting room at the Hotel was reserved for us, but just as Belcher was dictating his diary before dinner, in sailed Mother Seigel and her husband and several friends, saying beamingly 'They told us this was private, but we said "that's all right we know the people!"' Tableau!

Saturday [July 15]

A very early start by car to the foot of the Otira Gorge. None of us have ever been so cold in our lives. Instead of going over by coach, we had decided to walk – it's about 11 miles. O'Brien (our local Tommy Cocks – a terrible man who talks as though he has a hot potato in his mouth and breathes hard when he eats, and who Belcher hates more than he has hated any of our guides yet) did his best to dissuade us saying (a) it would

The coaches ready to
leave Arthur's pass for
Otiria Gorge.

be frozen and we should break our legs (b) it was too steep
(c) we should never do it in the time. He took our luggage by
the coach. It was a most glorious walk, mountains each side,
three miles up to the top then along over the saddle, and then
winding down through dark pine and fir trees with wonderful
icicles hanging from them. It was agreed by me and B. that
Archie should not be permitted to walk at his usual swinging
pace up hills – as a matter of fact I could beat Belcher up hill
any day! Several halts for photography, and finally we almost
ran the last mile down hill into Arthur's Pass so as to beat the
coach and 'snoo' O'Brien which we did by seven minutes. Quite
a comfortable journey on by train into Christchurch, and into
a comfortable Hotel once more, for which we were all devoutly
thankful.

OPPOSITE: 'Otiria
Gorge' and 'Agatha
and Belcher rounding
a corner'.

Icicles.

I found some beautiful violets in my room sent from a florist by order of Mrs Fordham, and a long letter from her, also a letter from her sister Mrs Wood asking me to tea on Sunday. After dinner we went out to a concert, Rosina Buckman and Maurice D'Oisley. 'Zealandia's Queen of Song' as a toothless old gentleman got up and called her.

Sunday [July 16]

A quiet morning of much needed mending! Went to tea with the Cecil Woods. They are charming, she is a sweet little thing, and he is an architect, and was most interesting about his work, and about his student days in Chelsea.

A delightful little impromptu morning tea was given yesterday by the members of the Committee of the Canterbury Women's Club, in honour of Mrs Christie, wife of Colonel Christie, a member of the British Empire Exhibition Mission. In a cordial little speech of welcome, Mrs Holland, president of the club, expressed her own and the members' pleasure at meeting Mrs Christie, and regretted that her stay in Christchurch was necessarily so brief. Mrs Christie, who is the author of several successful detective stories, thanked Mrs Holland for her kindly welcome, and spoke most enthusiastically of the scenic beauties of New Zealand, most particularly of the West Coast. Mrs Thacker, on behalf of the Mayor, presented Mrs Christie with a beautiful bouquet of orchids and maidenhair, the products of the Botanical Gardens. The guest of honour wore, over her mole coloured marocain frock, a charming loose Paisley wrap, with mole collar and a small mole hat of hatter's plush, with upturned brim trimmed with pastel tinted ribbons that toned with the wrap. The ladies present were Mrs Thacker, Mrs Holland, Miss Stoddart, Mrs R. T. Fosswill, Miss Orchard, Mrs S. C. Owen, Miss Raine, Mrs J. E. Russell, Mrs W. J. Jenkin, Mrs E. H. Wyles, Mrs W. J. Hunter, Mrs Schneider, and Mrs Claude Sawtell.

Archie, Agatha and Belcher (left), and an article from The Press, *Tuesday 18 July, 1922.*

Monday [July 17]

Was entertained by the Women's Club to morning tea –
rather alarming. Mrs Jenkin, a stout voluble lady, fetched
me and conducted me into a room simply full of women. I
was introduced all round, presented with a bouquet, and the
President, Mrs Holland got up and made a speech. Horror! I
too had to make a speech hanging on firmly to Mr Pecksniff's
advice 'Take care of the sounds and the sense will take care of

Christchurch Cathedral. itself.' Then the Mayor, Dr Thacker, came along, said I should

The river Avon in Christchurch.

have been at the Civic Reception and added the cheering information that he had 'spoken his mind plainly to your husband and Major Belcher'! (He is a reputed Bolshevist).

In the afternoon he called for me and took me to an Institute for old ladies where they are to consider themselves beneficiaries under a will, and there is no question of charity – rather a nice idea. There were a lot of them all sitting in a most magnificent drawing room round the fire knitting.

Tuesday [July 18]

A. went off to Invercargill this morning – right down south. I am going north to Rotorua by myself.

Love

Agatha

CHINA
Foo-Chow
Amoy
Canton
Hong-kong
Formosa Strait
Balington Channel
Ryukyu I.
Oshima
Shuri
RYUKYU Is.
(TO JAPAN)
Oshima
VOLCANO Is.
BONIN Is.
MARCUS I.
Tai-wan
TAIWAN
LOS JARDINES I.
Kiung-Chow
AINAN
HINA
Aparri
Luzon
MANILA
MINDORO I.
PHILIPPINE
MARIANNE OR
LADRONE
ISLANDS
FORMER GERMAN
SEA
PANAY I.
SAMAR I.
ISLANDS
EGOI Is.
GUAM I.
(U.S.)
ALAWAN I.
Sulu
Sea
MINDANAO
Cotabato
Sulu I.
CELEBES
SEA
PELEW Is.
CAROLINE ISLANDS
PONAPI I.
KUSAIE
Elopura
runei
RNEO
Pasir
GILOLO I.
GREENWICH I.
ADMINISTERED BY JAP
Geelvink B.
ADMIRALTY Is.
BISMARCK
ARCH.
NEW MECKLENBURG I.
FORMER GERMAN
BOUGAINVILLE
SOLOMON
Java Sea
Macassar
CELEBES
Boeroe I.
CERAM I.
BANDA SEA
AROE
Is.
NEW GUINEA
Pommern I.
New
Pommern
Choiseul
N. Georgia
ISABEL
ISLAN
MALAY
FLORIS SEA
FLORIS I.
FRED HENRY I.
SUMBAWA I.
ARAFURA SEA
Torres Strait
Guadalcanar
LOUISIADE
ARCH.
S. CH
RENNELL
ANDAL WOOD I.
TIMOR I.
BATHURST I.
C. York
Somerset
Chine Strait
ESPIRITU SANTO
MALLICOLLO
Cambridge G.
Darwin
Gulf of
Carpentaria
GREAT
BARRIER
Cooktown
CORAL SEA
C. Levequ
Normanton
NORTHERN
BARRIER
REEFS
Roeburn
W.
ape
WESTERN
TERRITORY
Bowen
Clermont
QUEENSLAND
NEW CALEDONIA
Noume
Carnarvon
L. Amandais
AUSTRALIA
SOUTH
Eyre L.
AUSTRALIA
Warwick
GR. SANDY I.
BRISBANE
garra
AUSTRALIA
L. Barlee
Paroo R.
L. Torrens
Darling R.
NEW
SOUTH WALES
Newcastle
LORD HOVE
ERTH
nburg
C.
euwin
Williamsburg
GREAT
AUSTRALIAN
BIGHT
Albany
Spencer G.
ADELAIDE
Lachlan R.
Murray R.
SYDNEY
CANBERRA
Kangaroo I.
Kingston
Portland
VICTORIA
Geelong
MELBOURNE
Cape Howe
Port Phillip
Bass Strait
FURNEAUX GROUP
Launceston
TASMANIA
N

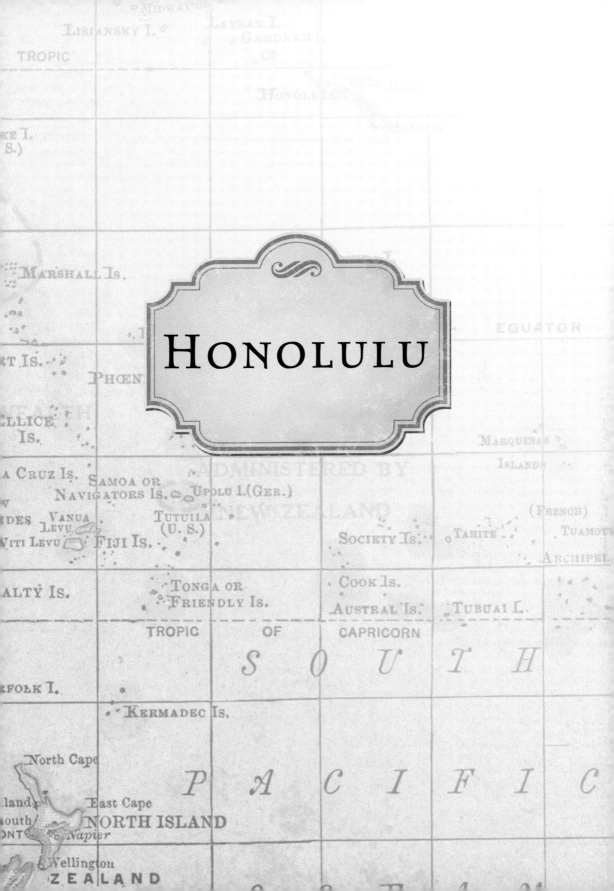

Honolulu

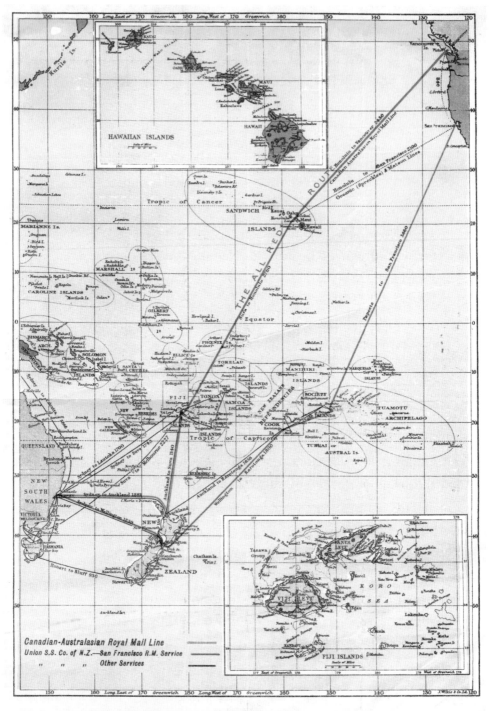

CHART OF ROUTE.—Canadian-Australasian Royal Mail Line.

UNION STEAM SHIP CO. OF NEW ZEALAND, Ltd., Managing Agents.

Belcher was pleased to be back in New Zealand. He had many friends there, and was happy as a schoolboy. When Archie and I left for Honolulu he gave us his blessing and urged us to enjoy ourselves. It was heaven for Archie to have no more work to do, no more contending with a crotchety and ill-tempered colleague. We had a lazy voyage, stopping at Fiji and other islands, and finally arrived at Honolulu. It was far more sophisticated than we had imagined with masses of hotels and roads and motor-cars. We arrived in the early morning, got into our rooms at the hotel, and straight away, seeing out of the window the people surfing on the beach, we rushed down, hired our surf-boards, and plunged into the sea. We were, of course, complete innocents. It was a bad day for surfing – one of the days when only the experts go in – but we, who had surfed in South Africa, thought we knew all about it. It is very different in Hono-lulu. Your board, for instance, is a great slab of wood, almost too heavy to lift. You lie on it, and slowly paddle yourself out towards the reef, which is – or so it seemed to me – about a mile away. Then, when you have finally got there, you arrange yourself in position and wait for the proper kind of wave to come and shoot

PREVIOUS PAGE:
Waikiki Beach, Honolulu.

you through the sea to the shore. This is not so easy as it looks. First you have to recognise the proper wave when it comes, and secondly, even more important, you have to know the *wrong* wave when it comes, because if *that* catches you and forces you down to the bottom. Heaven help you!

I was not as powerful a swimmer as Archie, so it took me longer to get out to the reef. I had lost sight of him by that time, but I presumed he was shooting into shore in a negligent manner as others were doing. So I arranged myself on my board and waited for a wave. The wave came. It was the wrong wave. In next to no time I and my board were flung asunder. First of all the wave, having taken me in a violent downward dip, jolted me badly in the middle. When I arrived on the surface of the water again, gasping for breath, having swallowed quarts of salt water, I saw my board floating about half a mile away from me, going into shore. I myself had a laborious swim after it. It was retrieved for me by a young American, who greeted me with the words: 'Say, sister, if I were you I wouldn't come out surfing today. You take a nasty chance if you do. You take this board and get right into shore now.' I followed his advice.

Before long Archie rejoined me. He too had been parted from his board. Being a stronger swimmer, though, he had got hold of it rather more quickly. He made one or two more trials, and succeeded in getting one good run. By that time we were bruised, scratched and completely exhausted. We returned our surf-boards, crawled up the beach, went up to our rooms, and fell exhausted on our beds. We slept for about four hours, but were still exhausted when we awoke. I said doubtfully to Archie: 'I

Agatha with her hired surf board.

suppose there is a great deal of pleasure in surfing?' Then sighing, 'I wish I was back at Muizenberg.'

The second time I took the water, a catastrophe occurred. My handsome silk bathing dress, covering me from shoulder to ankle was more or less torn from me by the force of the waves. Almost nude, I made for my beach wrap. I had immediately to visit the hotel shop and provide myself with a wonderful, skimpy, emerald green wool bathing dress, which was the joy of my life, and in which I thought I looked remarkably well. Archie thought I did too.

We spent four days of luxury at the hotel, and then had to look about for something cheaper. In the end we rented a small chalet on the other side of the road from the hotel. It was about half the price. All our days were spent on the beach and surfing, and little

by little we learned to become expert, or at any rate expert from the European point of view. We cut our feet to ribbons on the coral until we bought ourselves soft leather boots to lace round our ankles.

I can't say that we enjoyed our first four or five days of surfing – it was far too painful – but there were, every now and then, moments of utter joy. We soon learned, too, to do it the easy way. At least I did – Archie usually took himself out to the reef by his own efforts. Most people, however, had a Hawaiian boy who towed you out as you lay on your board, holding the board by the grip of his big toe, and swimming vigorously. You then stayed, waiting to push off on your board, until your boy gave you the word of instruction. 'No, not this, not this, Missus. No, no, wait – *now!*' At the word 'now' off you went, and oh, it was

The interior of the chalet.

heaven! Nothing like it. Nothing like that rushing through the water at what seems to you a speed of about two hundred miles an hour; all the way in from the far distant raft, until you arrived, gently slowing down, on the beach, and foundered among the soft flowing waves. It is one of the most perfect physical pleasures that I have known.

After ten days I began to be daring. After starting my run I would hoist myself carefully to my knees on the board, and then endeavour to stand up. The first six times I came to grief, but this was not painful – you merely lost your balance and fell off the board. Of course, you had lost your board, which meant a tiring swim, but with luck your Hawaiian boy had followed and retrieved it for you. Then he would tow you out again and you would once more try. Oh, the moment of complete triumph on the day that I kept my balance and came right into shore standing upright on my board!

We proved ourselves novices in another way which had

disagreeable results. We completely underestimated the force of the sun. Because we were wet and cool in the water we did not realise what the sun could do to us. One ought normally, of course, to go surfing in the early morning or late afternoon, but we went surfing gloriously and happily at midday – at noon itself, like the mugs we were – and the result was soon apparent. Agonies of pain, burning back and shoulders all night – finally enormous festoons of blistered skin. One was ashamed to go down to dinner in an evening dress. I had to cover my shoulders with a gauze scarf. Archie braved ribald looks on the beach and went down in his pyjamas. I wore a type of white shirt over my arms and shoulders. So we sat in the sun, avoiding its burning rays, and only cast off these outer garments at the moment we

Archie surfing in his pyjamas, and later once recovered.

Banana tree and waterfall.

went in to swim. But the damage was done by then, and it was a long time before my shoulders recovered. There is something rather humiliating about putting up one hand and tearing off an enormous strip of dead skin.

Our little chalet bungalow had banana trees all round it – but bananas, like pineapples, were a slight disappointment. I had imagined putting out a hand, pulling a banana off the stem and eating it. Bananas are not treated like that in Honolulu. They are a serious source of profit, and they are always cut down green. Nevertheless, even though one couldn't eat bananas straight off the tree one could still enjoy an enormous variety such as one had never known existed. I remember Nursie, when I was a child of three or four, describing bananas in India to me, and the difference between the plantains, which were large and uneatable, and the bananas which were small and delicious – or was it the other way about? Honolulu offered about ten varieties. There were red bananas, large bananas, small bananas called ice-cream bananas, which were white and fluffy inside, cooking bananas, and so on. Apple bananas were another flavour, I think. One became very choosy as to what one ate.

The Hawaiians themselves were also slightly disappointing. I had imagined them as exquisite creatures of beauty. I was slightly put off to begin with by the strong smell of coconut oil with which all the girls smeared themselves and a good many of them were not good-looking at all. The enormous meals of hot meat stews were not at all what one had imagined either. I had always thought that Polynesians lived mostly on delicious fruits of all kinds. Their passion for stewed beef much surprised me.

OVERLEAF: *‘Aloha to Honolulu!’*

Agatha.

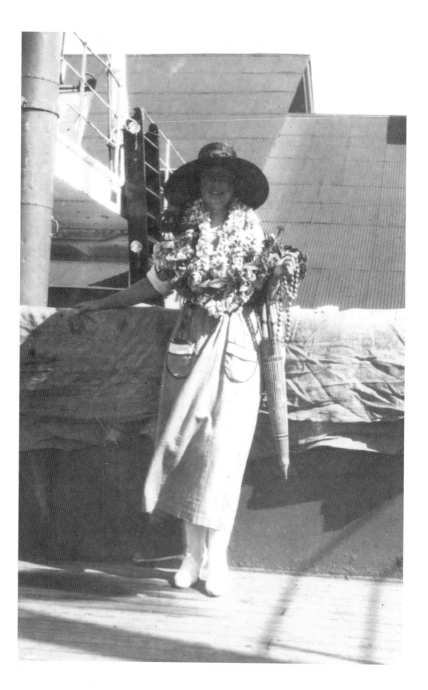

Archie.

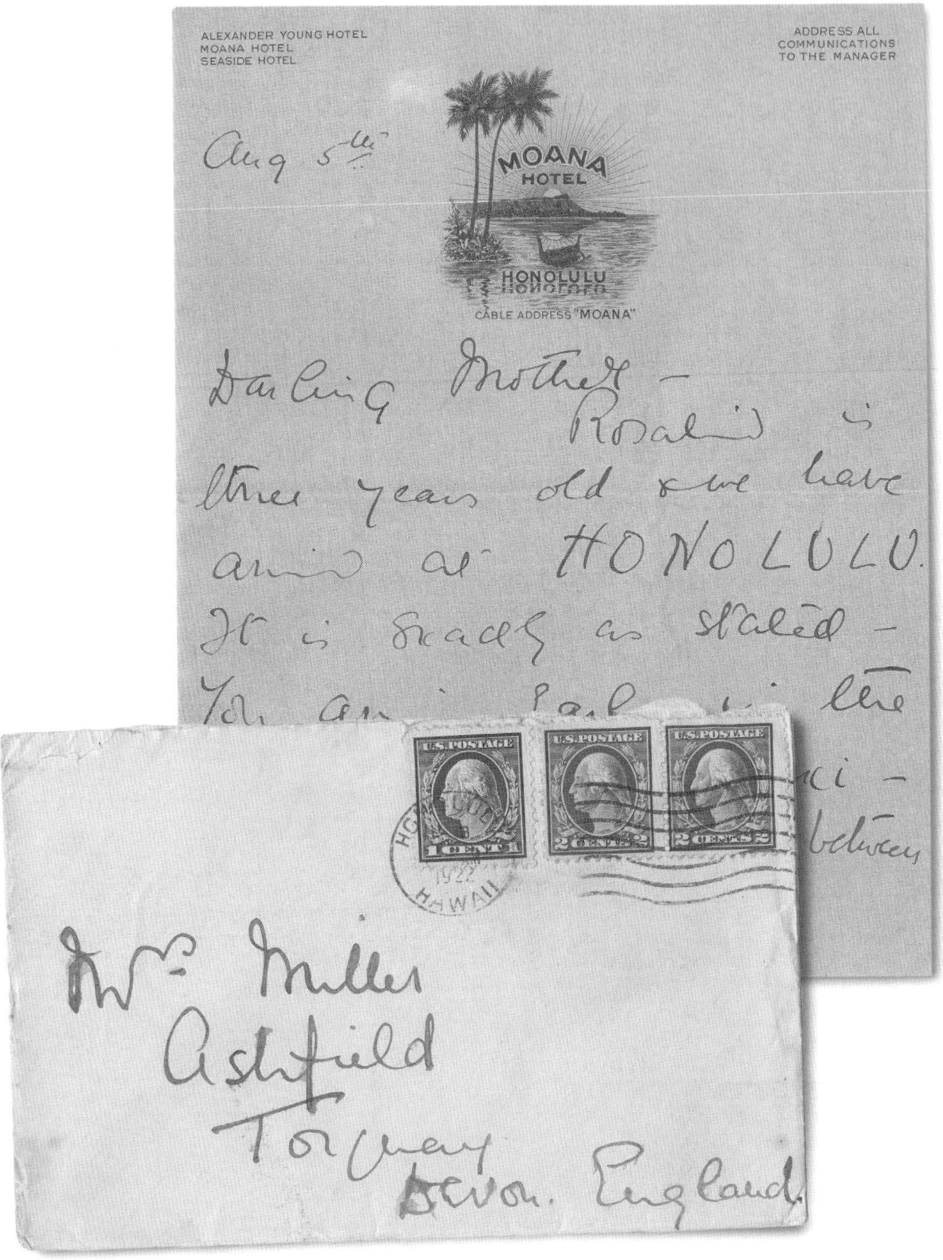
ALEXANDER YOUNG HOTEL
MOANA HOTEL
SEASIDE HOTEL
ADDRESS ALL
COMMUNICATIONS
TO THE MANAGER
Aug 5th
MOANA
HOTEL
HONOLULU
CABLE ADDRESS "MOANA"
Darling Mother -
Rosalind is
three years old & we have
arrived at HONOLULU.
It is exactly as stated -
U.S. POSTAGE
1922
HAWAII
Mrs Miller
Ashfield
Torquay
Devon. England.

Moana Hotel,
Honolulu

August 5 [Saturday]

Darling Mother

Rosalind is three years old and we have arrived at
HONOLULU. It is exactly as stated. You arrive early in the
morning, take a taxi, and go along a road between palms and
lovely flowers, hedges of hibiscus, red, pink, white, oleanders,
blue plumbago and great laburnum trees and poinsettias, like

*Moana Hotel and
Waikiki Beach.*

Canadian - Australasian Royal Mail Line.

R. M. S. "MAKURA."

R. CRAWFORD Commander.

Sailing from

SYDNEY | **AUCKLAND**
July 2oth. 1922. July 25th.

for

SUVA (Fiji) HONOLULU, VICTORIA (B.C.) and
VANCOUVER,

DUE

SUVA, | **HONOLULU,** | **VANCOUVER,**
July 29th. Aug, 5th. Aug 12th.

OFFICERS:

A. W. CREESE.........................First Officer
R. B. DENNISTON......................Second Officer
J. G. BOYD...........................Third Officer
T. DEE...............................Fourth Officer
C. LEIGHTON..........................Purser
R. G. WALLIS.........................Assistant Purser
C. A. EDWARDS........................Surgeon
J. HOWARTH...........................Chief Engineer
F. W. ERRINGTON......................Chief Steward
H. F. HARTLEY ....Wireless Operator
N. LEEDER...........Assistant Wireless Operator
M. MacGOWN.........Assistant Wireless Operator

laburnum but blood red – till you get to a green and white palace of a Hotel with a courtyard behind with a great banyan tree (which they light up at night with coloured lights) and the sea washing right up to the steps – with Hawaiians standing on great surf boards flashing in from the reef to the shore.

I forget where I was when I wrote last – was it first going to Rotorua? That was a wonderful place – the air full of sulphur fumes and boiling steam coming up from the ground and great quaking boiling mud pits and all the Maoris bathing and washing clothes in the hot pools. I was only there one day, but walked hard and saw a lot.

I was rather disappointed by Auckland – the 'Queen City', its being well laid out and all that – but the surroundings aren't

Washing clothes in hot pools in Rotorua.

Captain Crawford, and Archie's runner's up prize for gent's singles deck billiards.

Canadian-Australasian
Royal Mail Line

R. M. S. "MAKURA"

DECK SPORTS

SECOND PRIZE

Gents: Singles. Deck Billiards

WON BY

Col. Christie.

Crawford
Commander.

as grand as Wellington. We left on the Tuesday morning by the Makura – a nice boat with a nice Captain who is the champion quoits player of the Pacific – he takes on all the travellers at the sport and beats them! Nice people on board and a good passage on the whole, rather pitchy once or twice, but I was all right, though feeling pretty rotten as usual and unable to read or write. I still *hate* being on the sea!! Sastri, the Indian and his secretary were on board. Archie had met them at a dinner given for Sastri in Sydney and also in Auckland. They asked us to share a table. Sastri is a *wonderful* speaker – talks very little normally, seems

Agatha plays 'cutie'.

in a dream most of the time. Bajpai, his secretary, was a very clever and interesting little man – knows about any subject you cared to mention.

Lots of sports on board – quoits, gymkhana, fancy dress dance etc. I got as far as the semi final of the quoits and then fell to pieces. However, I beat the Captain one day which was a great triumph. Two nice people on board were the Taits who live on an island, Taviona in Fiji, and Fiona Cacanuti – she has just had a baby in Melbourne and is taking it back – 3 months old. We had a morning at Suva and enjoyed it – very hot and steamy

though, and unable to bathe because of sharks. The Fijians are wonderful. I'm glad we're staying here, not there. It's hot sun but a lovely fresh breeze, and the sea about 85.

Some of our friends off the boat are here. Two awfully nice boys just down from Oxford, Lord Swinfen and Mr St Aubyn, and two Australian sisters, Miss Morton and Mrs Minnett. We might have rather a good time together.

To be actually in Honolulu!

Lots of love

Agatha

On board the ship.

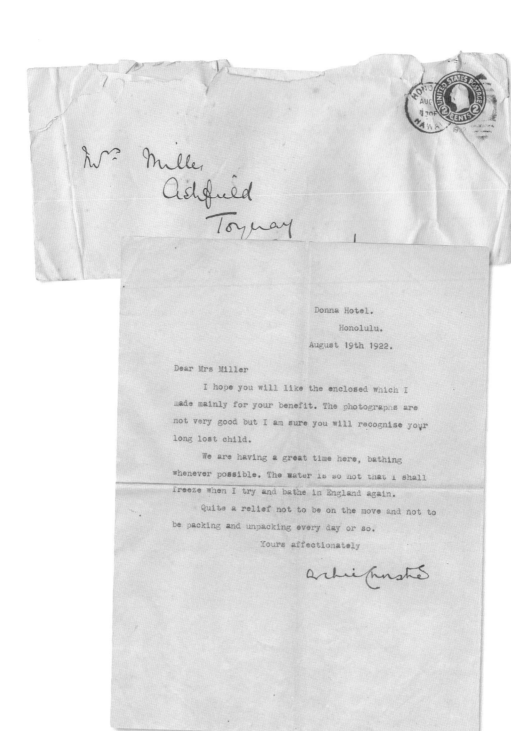

Donna Hotel.

Honolulu.

August 19th 1922.

Dear Mrs Miller

    I hope you will like the enclosed which I
made mainly for your benefit. The photographs are
not very good but I am sure you will recognise your
long lost child.

    We are having a great time here, bathing
whenever possible. The water is so hot that I shall
freeze when I try and bathe in England again.

    Quite a relief not to be on the move and not to
be packing and unpacking every day or so.

        Yours affectionately

          Archie Christie

August 19th 1922 [Saturday]

Dear Mrs Miller

I hope you will like the enclosed which I made mainly for your benefit. The photographs are not very good but I am sure you will recognise your long lost child.

We are having a great time here, bathing whenever possible. The water is so hot that I shall freeze when I try and bathe in England again.

Quite a relief not to be on the move and not to be packing and unpacking every day or so.

Yours affectionately

Archie Christie

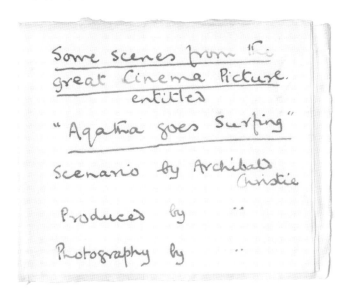

"Good morning"
Just finishing
my
breakfast
on the
Lanai'
no "mush" though'"

"I just
love my
little
bungalow
among the banana trees!"

iews

atha Christie, the well known novelist

" Every morning I leave
the Donna "

" And board a tram — I
mean a street car —
for Waikiki — "

This
is my
faithful
board "Fred"!

" Surfing is
very easy.
You just
push your board out
to Sea ~ "

on it till a wave Comes — "

till a wave comes —

" — And then Come in

on the wave ! "

"I must
introduce
you
to
my

Hawaian Instructor
in the art —"

"And — to let you
into a secret —
this is my new
Surf Suit!"

"Good bye!"

[undated]

My darling Mum

Still enjoying ourselves, though we've had our troubles!
The first days bathing so burnt us that we were in real agony!
Archie was much the worst. His skin came up in huge blisters
all over his back and shoulders and the backs of his legs. He
could hardly bear his clothes rubbing against it. There's such
a cool breeze all the time you don't realise the heat of the sun.
But the pavements and roads are red hot, if you have a hole in
your shoe or very thin soles you soon find you are giving an
imitation of ancient Anglo Saxons walking over the red hot
ploughshares. We have tried all remedies – annointing ourselves
with coconut oil, whitening, peroxide cream etc. Finally A.
has taken to bathing in pyjamas, to the intense amusement of
the natives who roll about in ecstasies of mirth! We now bathe
only in the early morning and about 4. The water is lovely, so
hot, you could stay in all day and never feel cold. Some days
there are no breakers at all, and they are never very big. Most
of the surfers go out to a place where there is a break in the reef
and get the waves there. I've been out once, towed by an H.G.
(abbreviation of Hawaian Gentleman). Literally 'towed' – he
goes on a board ahead and holds your board with his toes and
pulls it along! Then when you get out there, he pushes you when
a wave is coming. It's awfully hard to start yourself. Our jolly

Lord Swenfen and St Aubyn.

friend St Aubyn (an awfully nice lad) can't do it and no more can Archie, they go out for hours and lie on their boards and paddle desperately and come back physical wrecks drooping with fatigue! We have had quite a lovely time together, St Aubyn, Lord Swinfen, Mrs Minnett and Miss Morton and old New Zealand gentleman Mr Luckie and his wife who has very bad neuritis. We went to a hula hula dance one evening and out to Haleiwa in the north of the island where you go in glass bottomed boats and see the coral and the wonderful coloured fish. The mountain and inland scenery of the island is quite fine, but nothing to rave about. Not to compare with New Zealand, waving fields of green sugar cane and rather wonderful green

A picnic lunch.

shadows on the hills, but none of the colour and luxurious vegetation that one imagines in a tropical island. The beautiful part is the road out to Waikiki and the two residential valleys, the Nuuanu and Manoa, gardens on either side of the mass of great flowering trees and shrubs, scarlet and yellow, faint blue plumbago hedges and hibiscus and oleander of every shade. And wonderful palms.

There are also magnificent roads everywhere, tarred and oiled and a constant stream of motors – *everyone* has a motor! You hear them passing in a stream up till 3 in the morning. It is also pleasing to see nice looking, well dressed people again, after the plainness of the Colonies!! The Americans are amazingly efficient – the whole place is wonderfully well run. Most of the women are fascinating, nearly all of the men have an individual and fantastic taste in headgear, one size too small at least according to our ideas, and all the sailors have the funniest little tight round white caps! I see now where Winston Churchill's American blood comes out!! And Monty's choice for the Batch Batenger, do you remember?! The whole island is a mass of fortifications and huge barracks. I suppose it is their Heligoland. There are Japanese everywhere – all the servants and waiters and most of the shops. Their English is not good, and they never understand a word one says.

To return to personal matters, Swinfen and St Aubyn went on after five days en route for America and England and we missed them very much. We then decided that the Moano was all very well for a week but was ruinous for a longer period, so we hunted round. Mrs Minnett and Miss Morton have gone to

Japanese Gardens, Monalua.

another hotel near the Moano on the sea, a little cheaper – not much – and a great deal nastier, I think! We have come here, half way between the town and Waikiki, but on the trams, and have a little cottage to ourselves – bedroom, sitting room and bathroom, quite nice meals on an open veranda or 'lanai'. We spend all our time (a) on the beach, (b) in the town drinking ice cream sodas and buying new remedies and preventatives for sun burn. We have given up all idea of going on to San Francisco and shall wait here for the 'Niagara' and Belcher. We only pay 40 dollars a week here which is very cheap – the Moano is 15 a day and there doesn't seem to be any extras, owing to the ubiquitous ice water of Prohibition! Mr Luckie arranged for us to become members of the Country Club which is in the middle of hills with a golf course and a beautiful club house, very cool, where you can sit all day in a cosy chair if you feel like it.

Mr and Mrs Luckie and an avenue of King Palms.

Mr Luckie called for us in a car yesterday and took us over the pineapple factory, the largest in the world, an amazing place, machinery for everything, slicing, peeling, labelling etc. All the workers wear rubber gloves, and they have beautiful rooms upstairs, showers and bathrooms, rest rooms and a matron they can leave their children with. Mostly Japanese and Fillipinos and Chinese, no Hawaians though, far too much children of nature! There are big dining rooms where they can have 5c, 10c up to 30c meals.

As fruit, I'm rather disappointed in pineapples, they are not any better, if as good, as the ones you buy in London shops, partly, I suppose, because they are picked rather unripe and haven't had time to mature. The things that are gorgeous, both here and in Queensland are bananas! I never knew what a banana could be. The 'apple bananas' are the best, fat and white with an indescribable flavour. I'm spoilt for ever for bought bananas! Amongst good cookery I have had, veal cutlets and round balls of corn and small pieces of banana also fried, then whole bananas dipped in batter and fried and served with maple syrup. This is as an entrée before the joint and you begin very often with little bowls of fruit salad flavoured with chopped mint – Madge would like that, I think.

The Post Office Building.

The great custom that prevails with the servants here seems to be that you have your time and you never depart from it. At 5 minutes to 9 precisely there is a rap on the door and a voice says 'Room Boy'. He then enters and proceeds to do the room taking absolutely no notice of whether you have finished your toilet or not. If you keep the door fastened he remains outside tapping and repeating 'Room Boy' until in desperation you let him in. In the same way last Monday a Japanese lady walked into our little house and announced herself as 'Wa-shing'. It appeared to be the only word of English she knew. She took our bundle, scorned the proffered list and disappeared into the blue, walking in again at evening later with everything correct and the solitary remark '40 cents'.

The streets with all the kimonoed ladies shuffling along look very picturesque, also the Chinese women with their black trousers and little jackets.

Tell Rosalind I am bringing her a Chinese child for her family. Are the Teddys still alive?! I think of my little poppet such a lot and get more and more homesick for her. Tell her poor Daddy went out to bathe in the sun again yesterday thinking he was sufficiently hardened and now he is all red and sore again. It is like 'the spots', he must just 'stroke them'. But he will soon be able to say 'Better Now.'

Lots of love, Mummy darling, and to Monty and Madge and Jane and my Joe-Joe – there is a dog at night barks like him, a tenor dog!

Your loving

Agatha

Agatha relaxing
on the beach.

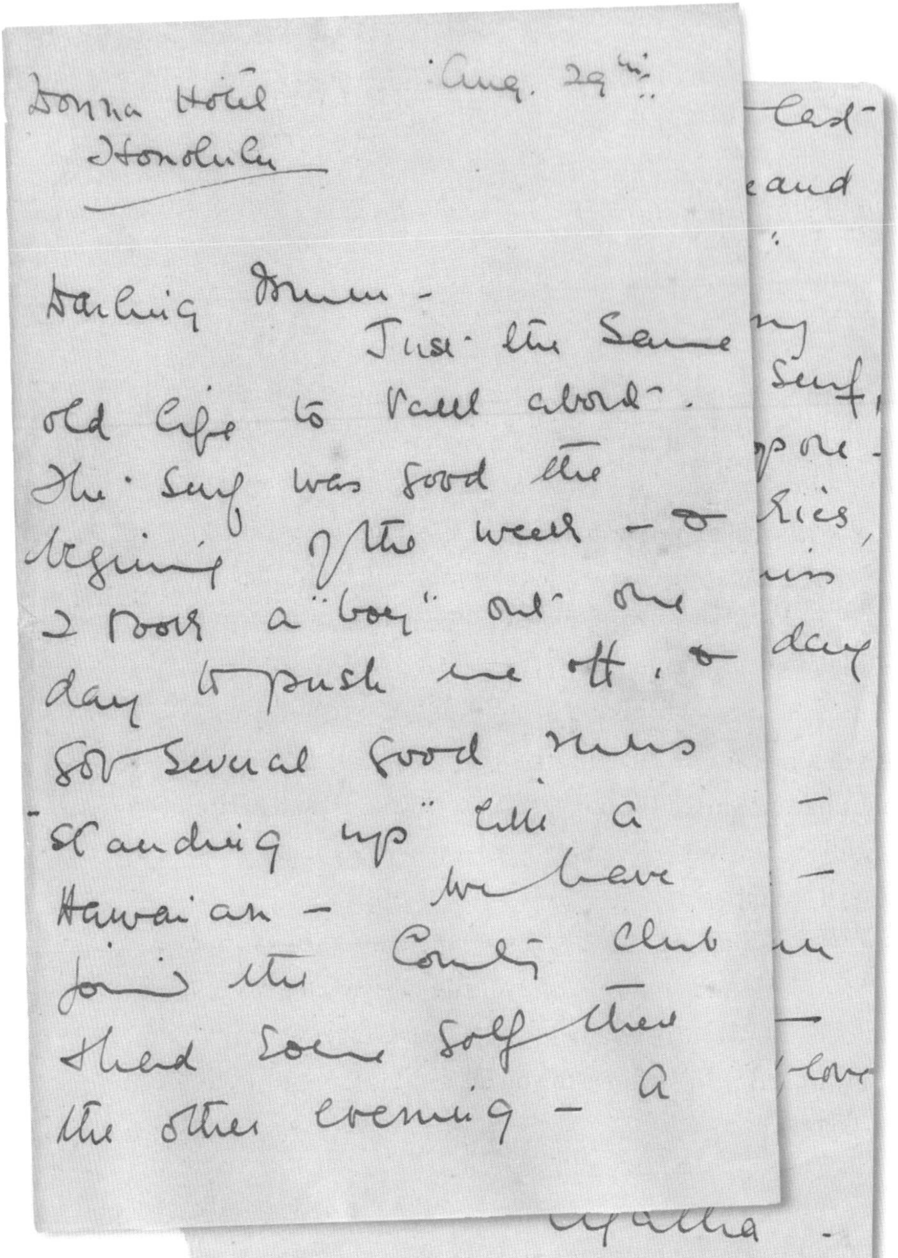

Donna Hotel
Honolulu

Aug. 29th

Darling Donna —
Just the same
old life to tell about.
The surf was good the
beginning of the week — I
took a "boy" out one
day to push me off, &
got several good runs
"standing up" like a
Hawaian — We have
joined the Country Club &
had some golf there
the other evening — A

led -
and
my
surf,
ore
Rics,
his
day
—
—
—
—
love
Agatha -

August 29th [Tuesday]

Darling Mum

Just the same old life to talk about. The surf was good the beginning of the week and I took a 'boy' out one day to push me off and got several good runs 'standing up' like a Hawaian. We have joined the Country Club and had some golf the other evening, a tremendous shower of 'liquid sunshine' came down from the mountains and wet us to the skin – and Archie has now got a bad cold! Also he stayed in the sea too long the beginning of the week and he's all blistered up and peeled again – back and shoulders nearly raw again. And I have got a sort of neuritis or strain in my left arm, can hardly move it and aches terribly. I haven't surfed the last two days it's disappeared again. You 'paddle' with your arms very vigorously when you surf, and that does it, I suppose.

Our friends the Luckies, also Mrs Minnett and Miss Morton left on Saturday on the return of the Mazussi for Sydney. We shall miss them. We've had rather fun in the sea together.

Really no news, lots of love to you all.

Love

Agatha

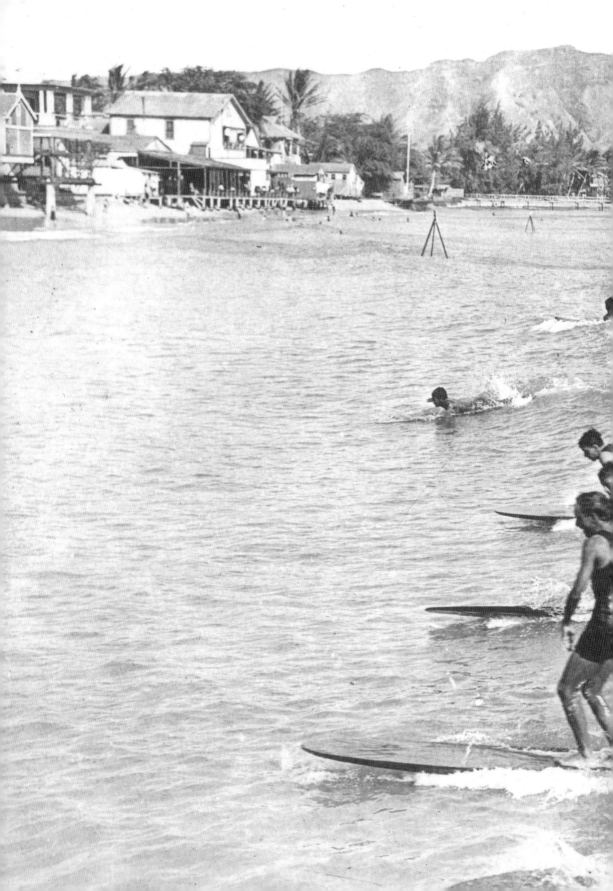

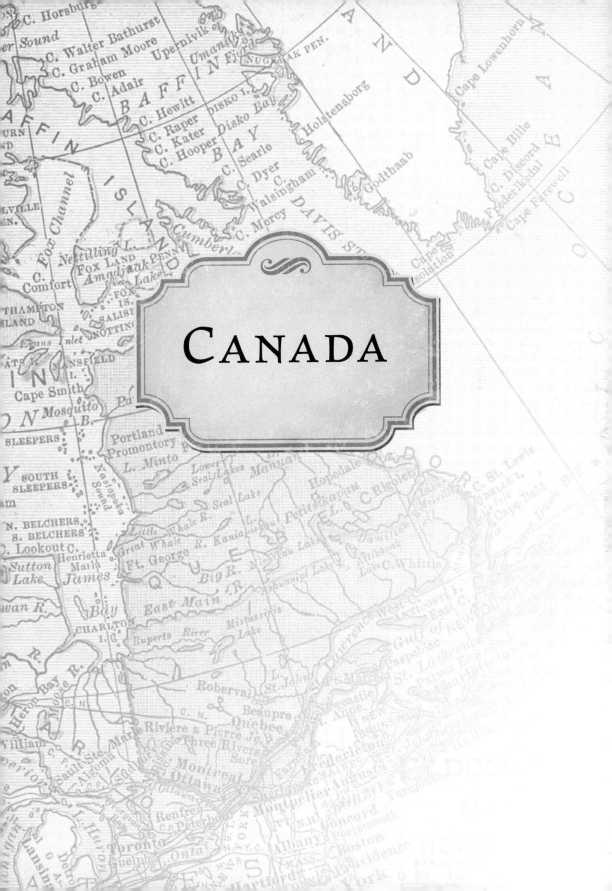

CANADA

Our holiday drew to a close, and we sighed a good deal at the thought of resuming our servitude. We were also growing slightly apprehensive financially. Honolulu had proved excessively expensive. Everything you ate or drank cost about three times what you thought it would. Hiring your surf-board, paying your boy – everything cost money. So far we had managed well, but now the moment had come when a slight anxiety for the future entered our minds. We had still to tackle Canada, and Archie's £1000 was dwindling fast. Our sea fares were paid for already so there was no worry over that. I could get to Canada, and I could get back to England. But there were my living expenses during the tour across Canada. How was I going to manage? However, we pushed this worry out of our minds and continued to surf desperately whilst we could. Much too desperately, as it happened.

I had been aware for some time of a bad ache in my neck and shoulder and began to be awakened every morning about five o'clock with an almost unbearable pain in my right shoulder and arm. I was suffering from neuritis, though I did not yet call

it by that name. If I'd had any sense at all I should have stopped using that arm and given up surfing, but I never thought of such a thing. There were only three days to go and I could not bear to waste a moment. I surfed, stood up on my board, displayed my prowess to the end. I now could not sleep at night at all because of the pain. However, I still had an optimistic feeling that it would go away as soon as I left Honolulu and had stopped surfing. How wrong I was. I was to suffer neuritis, and almost unendurable pain, for the next three weeks to a month.

Belcher was far from beneficent when we met again. He appeared to grudge us our holiday. Time we did some work, he said. 'Hanging about all this time, doing nothing. My goodness! It's extraordinary the way this thing has been fitted out, paying people to do nothing all the time!' He ignored the fact that he himself had had a good time in New Zealand and was regretting leaving his friends.

Since I was continually in pain, I went to see a doctor. He was not at all helpful. He gave me some ferocious ointment to rub into the hollow of my elbow when the pain was really bad. It must have been capsicum, I presume; it practically burnt a hole in my skin, and didn't do the pain much good. I was thoroughly miserable by now. Constant pain gets one down. It started every morning early. I used to get out of bed and walk about, since that seemed to make the pain more bearable. It would go off for an hour or two, and then come back with redoubled vigour.

At least the pain took my mind off our increasing financial worries. We were really up against it now. Archie was practically at the end of his £1000, and there was still over three weeks to go.

BRITISH TRADE MISSION
HERE FROM AUSTRALIA

Touring World to Arouse Interest and Support For Great London Industrial Exposition, Party Headed By Major E. A. Belcher Arrives on S.S. Niagara.

The British trade delegation which is touring the world in the interests of the British Empire Exhibition to be held in London in 1924, was greeted in Victoria on the arrival of the Canadian- Australasian liner Niagara this afternoon.

The mission is headed by Major E. A. Belcher, C.B.E., M.A., and the party includes Mr. and Mrs. Hiam, Colonel A. Christie, C.M.G., D.S.O., manager of the Bank of England, and Mrs. Christie, and F. W. Bates, the manager's secretary.

The members of the mission are on a world tour to arouse interest in and support for the display of Empire industry now being prepared in London at Wembley Park, which will be opened in 1924.

To Speak Here.

The Exhibition mission anticipates meeting local business men with a view to securing their co-operation as exhibitors, but is more interested in explaining to the general public the objective aimed at by the Prince of Wales and his collabrators in organizing the display of Empire industry, and securing a world-wide pilgrimage to London.

To aid the mission in this undertaking, the Chamber of Commerce has been asked to arrange for the holding of public meetings which may be addressed by the distinguished visitors.

Welcomed At William Head.

A party of Victoria business men left the city early to-day for William Head, where they boarded the Niagara and extended the city's greetings to the visitors. The party included J. W. Spencer, president of the Chamber of Commerce; C. T. Cross, chairman of the reception committee; Capt. T. J. Goodlake, local secretary of the Canadian Manufacturers' Association, and H. Cuthbertson, representing the Glasgow Chamber of Commerce, who is also on this coast for the purpose of promoting trade within the Empire.

When the liner docked at Pier 2 Premier Oliver and representatives of the Chamber of Commerce met the visitors. This afternoon they will visit the various points of interest in and around the city and to-morrow they will be entertained at Butchart's Gardens.

On Monday the visitors will be the guests of the Provincial Government on a tour of inspection of some of the industries in the neighborhood.

Luncheon.

On Tuesday at noon a luncheon will be given at the Hudson's Bay restaurant in honor of the guests, at which, owing to the limited space, accommodation will be provided for seventy-five. Tickets may be secured at the offices of the Chamber of Commerce, Belmont Building. The party will make further investigations on Tuesday in connection with their work and during their stay in the city an open meeting will be held at which Major Belcher will explain the exhibition project and the part the Province of British Columbia will be expected to play in it.

Hopes Canada Will Respond.

"Never before has there been a scientific effort to make a full survey of all the resources of the British Empire and to find means of putting them to the best uses for all of us," said Major Belcher to The Times on arrival here.

The mission hopes that Canada will respond to the idea with the same enthusiasm that Australia is doing and that all portions of the Empire will join hands in making the 1924 British Trade Exhibition in London something that will have a lasting moral effect as well as serving to promote closer trade relations.

The mission will interview all Provincial Governments in Canada with a view to securing some sort of inter-provincial conference at the end of the mission to settle the final details of Canada's participation in the exhibition.

"The idea has caught the imagination of Australia and that country is making a magnificent response, due largely to their sense of vision as to what the Exhibition will mean for the extension of Australia's trade," said Major Belcher.

A souvenir from Canada.

CANADA'S NEW COAT OF ARMS

BY PROCLAMATION OF HIS MAJESTY THE KING
DECEMBER 17TH, 1921.

"O Canada"

O Canada, our heritage, our love,
Thy worth we praise all other lands above.
From sea to sea, throughout thy length,
    from pole to borderland.
At Britain's side, whate'er betide, unflinchingly
    we'll stand.
With heart we sing, "God Save the King,"
"Guide Thou the Empire wide," do we
    implore,
"And prosper Canada from shore to shore."

We decided that the only thing was that I should forego travelling to Nova Scotia and Labrador and instead get myself to New York as soon as the money ran out. Then I could live with Aunt Cassie or May while Archie and Belcher were inspecting the silver fox industry.

Even then things were not easy. I could afford to stay in the hotels, but it was the *meals* that were so expensive. However, I hit on quite a good plan: I would make breakfast my meal. Breakfast was a dollar – at that time about four shillings in English money. So I would have breakfast down in the restaurant, and I would have everything that was on the menu. That, I may say, was a good deal. I had grapefruit, and sometimes pawpaw as well. I had buckwheat cakes, waffles with maple syrup, eggs and bacon. I came out from breakfast feeling like an overstuffed boa constrictor. But I managed to make that last until evening.

We had been given several gifts during our stay in the Dominions: a lovely blue rug for Rosalind with animals on it, which I was looking forward to putting in her nursery, and various other things – scarves, a rug, and so on. Among these gifts was an enormous jar of meat extract from New Zealand. We had carried this along with us, and I was thankful now that we had, for I could see that I was going to depend on it for sustenance. I wished heartily that I had flattered the Dehydrator to the extent that he would have pressed large quantities of dehydrated carrots, beef, tomatoes, and other delicacies upon me.

When Belcher and Archie departed to their Chambers of Commerce dinners, or wherever they were dining officially, I would retire to bed, ring the bell, say I was not feeling well, and ask for an enormous jug of boiling water as a remedy for my indigestion. When this came I would add some meat extract to it and nourish myself on that until the morning. It was a splendid jar, and lasted me about ten days. Sometimes, of course, I was asked out to luncheons or dinners too. Those were the red letter days. I was particularly fortunate in Winnipeg, where the daughter of one of the civic dignitaries called for me at my hotel and took me out to lunch at a very expensive hotel. It was a glorious meal. I accepted all the most substantial viands that were offered me. She ate rather delicately herself. I don't know what she thought of my appetite.

I think it was at Winnipeg that Archie went with Belcher on a tour of grain elevators. Of course, we should have known that anyone with a sinus condition ought never to go near a grain elevator, but I suppose it didn't occur to him or to me. He returned that day, his eyes streaming, and looking so ill that I was thoroughly alarmed. He managed the journey the next day as far as Toronto, but once there he collapsed completely, and it was out of the question for him to continue on the tour.

Belcher, of course, was in a towering rage. He expressed no sympathy. Archie was letting him down, he said. Archie was young and strong, it was all nonsense to go down like this. Yes, of course, he knew Archie had a high temperature. If he had such poor health he ought never to have come. Now Belcher was left to hold the baby all by himself. Bates was no use, as anyone knew. Bates was only of use for packing one's clothes, and even then he packed them all wrong. He couldn't fold trousers the right way, silly fool.

Bow River Valley, Banff.

I called in a doctor, advised by the hotel, and he pronounced that Archie had congestion of the lungs, must not be moved, and could not be fit for any kind of land of activity for at least a week. Fuming, Belcher took his departure, and I was left, with hardly any money, alone in a large, impersonal hotel, with a patient who was by now delirious. His temperature was over 103. Moreover, he came out with nettlerash. From head to foot he was covered with it, and suffered agony from the irritation, as well as the high fever.

It was a terrible time, and I am only glad now that I have forgotten the desperation and loneliness. The hotel food was not suitable, but I went out and got him invalid diet: a barley water, and thin gruel, which he quite liked. Poor Archie, I have never seen a man so maddened by what he went through with that appalling nettlerash. I sponged him all over, seven or eight times a day, with a weak solution of bicarbonate of soda and water, which gave him some relief. The third day the doctor suggested calling in a second opinion. Two owlish men stood on either side of Archie's bed, looking serious, shaking their heads, saying it was a grave case. Ah well, one goes through these things. A morning came when Archie's temperature had dropped, his nettlerash was slightly less obtrusive, and it was clear he was on the way to recovery. By this time I was feeling as weak as a kitten, mainly, I think, owing to anxiety.

In another four or five days Archie was restored to health, though still slightly weak, and we rejoined the detestable Belcher. I forget now where we went next; possibly Ottawa, which I loved. It was the fall, and the maple woods were beautiful. We stayed in a

Chateau Lake Louise.

private house with a middle-aged admiral, a charming man who had a most lovely Alsatian dog. He used to take me out driving in a dog-cart through the maple trees.

After Ottawa we went to the Rockies, to Lake Louise and Banff. Lake Louise was for a long time my answer when I was asked which was the most beautiful place I had ever seen: – a great, long, blue lake, low mountains on either side, all of a most glorious shape, closing in with snow mountains at the end of it. At Banff I had a great piece of luck. My neuritis was still giving me a lot of pain and I resolved to try the hot sulphur waters which many people assured me might do good. Every morning I soaked myself in them. It was a kind of swimming pool, and by going up to one end of it you could get the hot water as it came out of the spring, smelling powerfully of sulphur. I ran this on to the back of my neck and shoulder. To my joy, by the end of four days my neuritis left me for all practical purposes, for good. To be free of pain once more was an unbelievable pleasure.

OVERLEAF: *Bates, Belcher, Archie and Agatha at the hot sulphur swimming pool.*

EMPRESS HOTEL
VICTORIA, B/C.

September 17th [Sunday]

My darling Mummy

    The last Dominion!! It was delicious coming into Victoria
yesterday afternoon, blue sea and sunshine, crisp but not cold,
and a wonderful scent of pinewoods! A Mr Goss came with the
Premier and others to welcome us, and found he was a friend of
Blanche Dewdney's, does all her business out here for her, being
a lawyer. We were taken last night to the big observatory, the

Empress Hotel, Victoria.

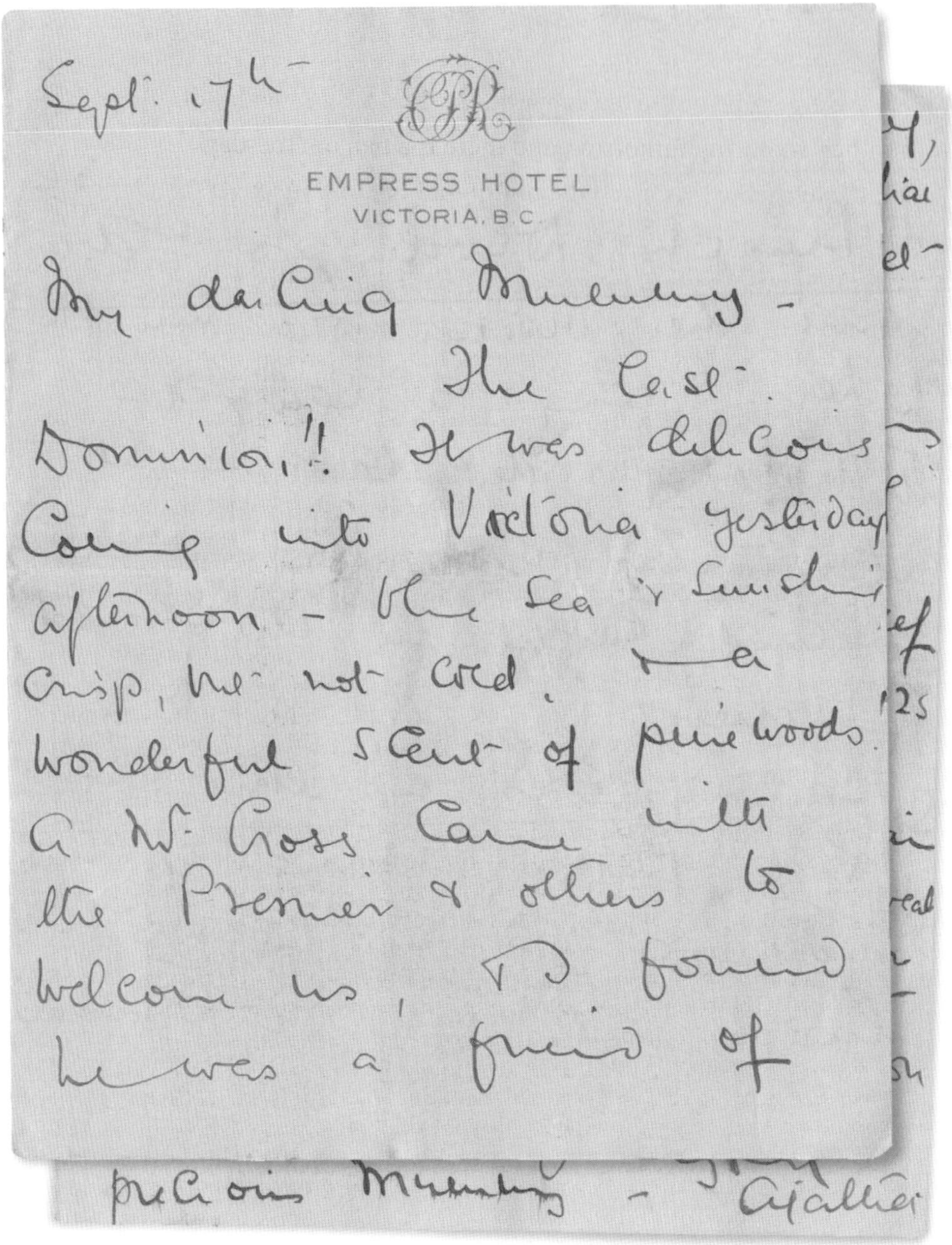

Sept. 17th

EMPRESS HOTEL
VICTORIA, B.C.

My darling Mummy —

The last —
Dominion!! It was delicious
coming into Victoria yesterday
afternoon — the sea & sunshine
crisp, but not cold. & a
wonderful scent of pine woods.
a Mr Gross came with
the Premier & others to
welcome us, & D. found
he was a friend of

precious Mummy — your Agather

second largest in the world, I believe, quite a big party of us in the cars. Lady Barnard rang up this morning and I am going to lunch with her on Tuesday.

We are going out to tea supper today and for a long day of 'lumber' motoring tomorrow, and there is a ball on Tuesday night, after which we catch the midnight boat to Vancouver. I may stay on here a day or two as I would like to see Kitty who is coming into Victoria to see Lëst off to England on the 19th (Tuesday). She suggests I should go back with her, stay a day or two when she goes home on the 23rd. But I would rather go on to Banff (right up in the Rockies!) with the others on the 24th. From there we go on through Calgary, Edmonton, Regina, Winnipeg and Toronto, stopping just 2 days in each city. From Toronto we are going for a weekend to Niagara Falls. That will be the 14th October. From there I could go to New York perhaps stay a week with Aunt Cassie and come home. The others go

Kitty, her elusive husband Lëst and their dog at home.

The hydro glider 'The Tortoise' at Victoria.

from Niagara to Ottawa (Dominion Capital) for a week, as that, of course, is the most important Government there, Governor General etc. I think I shall probably go with them and then on to Montreal. From Montreal they go on to Newfoundland, Nova Scotia etc. I don't want to do that much, Montreal is no great distance from Boston. I might stay there with them and then to New York and Aunt Cassie, and then home. Either by the same boat as the others (they sail from New York) but more probably an earlier one. Then I can have a nice long time with you before I have to set about getting the flat straight – servant etc. I am writing to Whitely to let the flat on for another 2 months up to the New Year. I fancy Belcher and Archie will only be home just before Xmas. If I do my 2nd plan, e.g. Montreal, Boston, New York, I should be home end of November. *If you want me home earlier, I can come.* I can come right away any time. Send me a wire and I'll come right through. I could be home in *ten days*. Of course we haven't got our mail yet, it's waiting for us at Vancouver, probably a *lot* of letters!! The last ones Belcher brought on from New Zealand, and they of course were nearly 2 months old. At Vancouver I shall get quite recent news. Both you and Madgie write *lovely* letters to me. I read them over and over again. My baby must be *so* sweet. I'm dying to see her, so is Archie! Haven't heard much of Joe-Joe lately? My own long nosed one. Madge wrote me *very* funny letters about Rip and Macauley and Cuckoo etc. Dear old Mont, I wish I'd been there for his birthday.

By the way, what about Shebani? Hadn't he better stay on? He understands Monty and the Sandfords have swallowed him. I suspect they have given notice again when Cuckoo arrived, but I'm beginning to have great faith now in their always ultimately reconsidering it!

I can pay Shebani's wages. I've got far more money now than I ever dreamed I should have after this trip. My March a/c from John Lane is £47 for 'Swedish Rights' and things like that off '*Styles*'. I shall get a good lot of Tommy & Tuppence money this September, and all my dividends are pouring in at home. So do do what you'd like about S.

I've told John Lane to send money out here to Vancouver, also the short Poirots and other stories. He has advised against publication of latter (as I thought he would) so that counts as a book, so the next I write will be the *5th*! I heard from Dodd Mead & Co that it was being published in New York June 17th. I shall go and see them when I am there. Also Freda Steinberg (my Australian journalist friend) gave me letters to 2 journalist

Programme for the ship's concert in which Agatha performed.

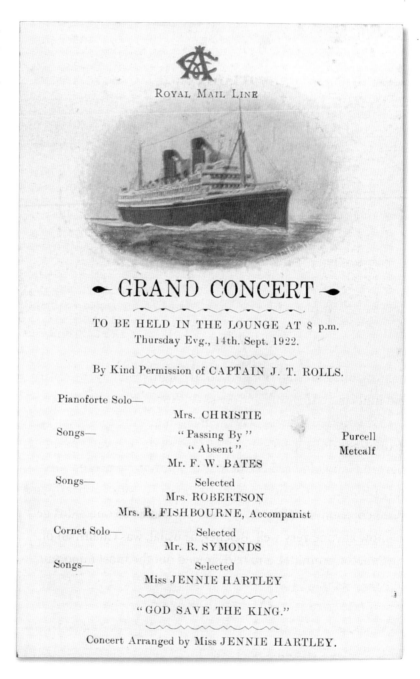

ROYAL MAIL LINE

➤ GRAND CONCERT ➤

TO BE HELD IN THE LOUNGE AT 8 p.m.
Thursday Evg., 14th. Sept. 1922.

By Kind Permission of CAPTAIN J. T. ROLLS.

Pianoforte Solo—
Mrs. CHRISTIE

Songs—   "Passing By"   Purcell
                           "Absent"   Metcalf
Mr. F. W. BATES

Songs—   Selected
Mrs. ROBERTSON
Mrs. R. FISHBOURNE, Accompanist

Cornet Solo—   Selected
Mr. R. SYMONDS

Songs—   Selected
Miss JENNIE HARTLEY

"GOD SAVE THE KING."

Concert Arranged by Miss JENNIE HARTLEY.

friends of hers in New York and they might give me some help and hints in getting some of the short stories published.

My writing is getting scratchy!!! I am beginning my diary again now, so the *next* letter will be typewritten. I gave up the diary at Honolulu because there was nothing to say every day but 'went surfing'! And if I write on boats I'm sick at once. Quite nice people on the Niagara. It was only a week so one didn't get to know anyone very well. Belcher, as usual, was Chairman of the Sports Committee and had singled out the most important lady on the boat, Mrs Lionel Atwill, who I gather is a very famous American actress, acted with Tree when he was over, She's a charming person, a shade bored by Belcher, but he has the good old 'Melland' touch and hangs on like grim death. He really has been quite pleasant and reasonable for a long time now, not having had to be teetotal! He and I won the bridge tournament together.

The day before leaving Honolulu I was stricken with a bad pain in the neck and shoulder. I thought perhaps I'd ricked it, but at last I had the doctor, quite a good one, a real one on a holiday, not an old ship's one, and he said it was neuritis. He gave me some stuff to take and I think it's getting better, but it's like sciatica, you get terrible bouts of pain when you least suspect them, it's like toothache all down your arm.

Considering that people go to Honolulu for the heat and sea water to do their neuritis good, it seems a little hard!! But I'm getting the pain much less often now. I've only been here a day, but I *do* like the Canadians. So smart and tall and well set up and not nearly so 'provincial'. Also there seems a lot more 'entertaining' going about. A good thing when a slice of beef for dinner costs you $1.25 and a potato 40c!!!

Don't seem to have Memam's address with me. It's Commonwealth Avenue, but I can't remember the number. If I want it in a hurry I'll cable you.

Lots and lots and lots of love my precious Mummy.

Yours

Agatha

Cowichan Lake

Postmark: Victoria, BC, Sep 21, 1922

We motored here on Monday.

Cowichan Lake

A day with the Island Lumber Co.
Victoria B.C.

Leaving the car -

On the train -

Arriving
in
the Car.

Agatha   Mr Olliver
          Mr Duncan.

Avenue chats with
          Premier Olliver

B.C. Parliament Buildings

Postmark: Victoria, B.C., Sep 21, 1922

We had our open air meeting here on Monday night.

ILLUMINATION OF B. C. PARLIAMENT BUILDINGS

CANADIAN PACIFIC HOTELS
BANFF SPRINGS HOTEL,
BANFF, ALTA

September 25th [Monday]

My darling little Pet,

What a lovely book you sent me for my birthday, and you coloured the pictures all by yourself. You *are* a *clever* Baba. You did them just beautifully and Mummy is so pleased. I shall be coming home very soon now to see my little Rosalind. Good Grandma to teach you to wave to 'Mummy-Daddy-across-the-

CPR Hotel, Banff Springs.

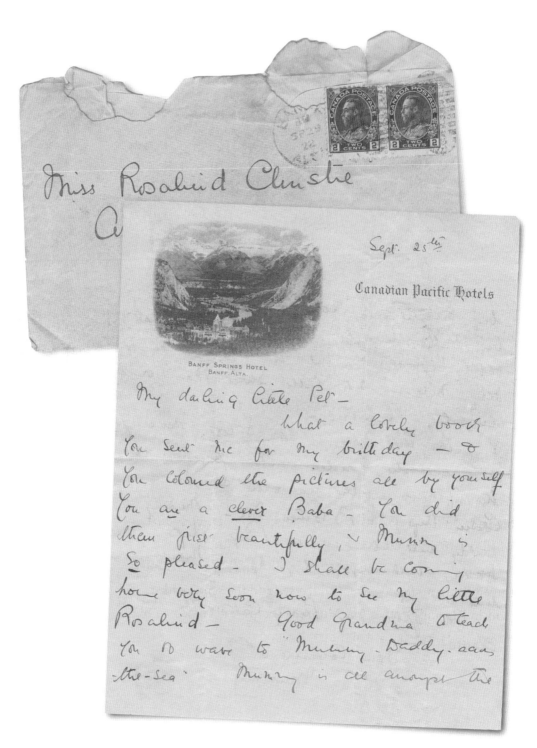

Miss Rosalind Christie

Sept. 25th

Canadian Pacific Hotels

BANFF SPRINGS HOTEL
BANFF, ALTA.

My darling Little Pet —

What a lovely book
You sent me for my birthday — &
You coloured the pictures all by yourself
You are a _clever_ Baba — You did
them just beautifully, & Mummy is
_so_ pleased — I shall be coming
home very soon now to see my little
Rosalind — Good Grandma to teach
You to wave to "Mummy - Daddy - across
-the-sea" Mummy is all amongst the

Banff.

sea.' Mummy is all amongst the big mountains now. There are big baths in the rocks full of hot bubbling water, but it doesn't smell very nice, not like Sweet Peas or Auntie Punkie.

You will have a lot to tell Mummy all about the garden and the pigeons and the flowers, and the sea and the sands and Cousin Rip and Brother Joe. Mummy-Daddy will come in a Big Ship, Daddy will enjoy it and poor Mummy will be ill.

Lots of love, my Pussy Cat. You are a clever girl.

Your loving

Mummy

BOW VALLEY, BANFF

Postmark: Calgary, Alta, Oct 1, 1922, 1.30pm

Murder on the Links is coming out in the 'Grand' – begins
October or November I believe. Lovely lots of letters waiting for
us at Vancouver – I shall be home end of November for certain.
AC.

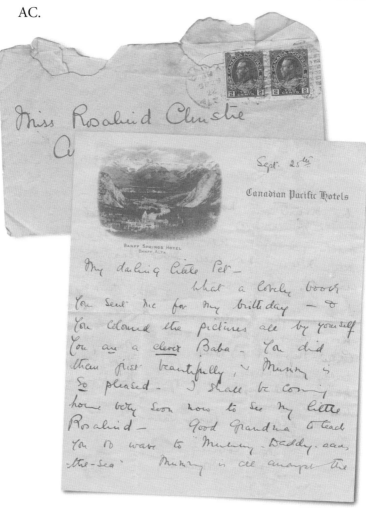

BRITISH MISSION TO VISIT PRINCE OF WALES' RANCH

Final Arrangements for Their Entertainment Will Be Completed Wednesday

A visit to the Prince of Wales ranch will be one of the chief items of interest during the two-day visit of the British Empire Exhibition mission, which will arrive in Calgary from Banff, on Thursday afternoon, at 2:05 o'clock. Before leaving on their round-the-world tour, Colonel Belcher, M.B.E., who is in charge of the mission was specially requested by the Prince of Wales to pay his Alberta ranch a visit during his stop-over in Calgary, and it is stated that Professor W. L. Carlyle has made arrangements to entertain the party at the ranch though the time of the visit has not yet been decided upon.

Following a civic reception at the depot, the party will be taken for a drive around the city. Just what other form of entertainment will be provided on behalf of the city will not be settled until Wednesday afternoon, when the reception committee will meet and complete the details. The meeting is called for 4 o'clock in the city hall.

Col. Belcher will address the members of the Board of Trade at luncheon, on Friday, and it is probable that a dinner will be tendered the party on Friday evening, in the Palliser hotel.

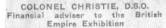

British Empire Exhibition Mission Arrives in Edmonton

COLONEL CHRISTIE, D.S.O.
Financial adviser to the British Empire Exhibition

MAJOR E. A. BELCHER, C.B.E.
Assistant-general manager of the British Empire Exhibition

'Starting for the Prince's Ranch, Belcher and Professor Carlyle' (top).

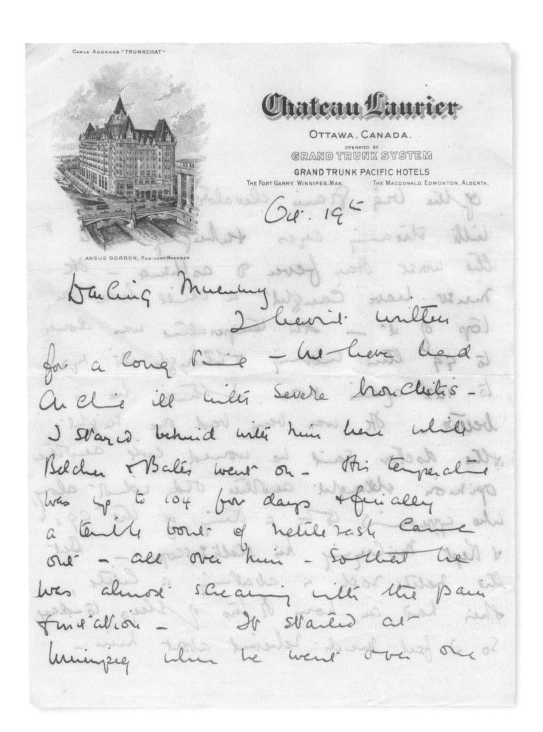

Cable Address "TRUNKCHAT"

Chateau Laurier

OTTAWA, CANADA.

OPERATED BY

GRAND TRUNK SYSTEM

GRAND TRUNK PACIFIC HOTELS

THE FORT GARRY, WINNIPEG, MAN.   THE MACDONALD, EDMONTON, ALBERTA.

ANGUS GORDON, RESIDENT MANAGER.

Oct. 19ᵗʰ

Darling Mummy

I haven't written
for a long time — We have had
Archie ill with severe bronchitis —
I stayed behind with him here while
Belcher & Bates went on — His temperature
was up to 104 for days & finally
a terrible bout of nettlerash came
out — all over him — so that he
was almost screaming with the pain
& irritation — It started at
Winnipeg when he went over one of

October 19th [Thursday]

Darling Mummy

I haven't written for a long time, we have had Archie ill with severe bronchitis. I stayed behind with him here while Belcher and Bates went on. His temperature was up to 104 for days and finally a terrible bout of nettle rash came out, all over him, so that he was almost screaming with the pain and irritation. It started in Winnipeg when he went over one of the big grain elevators and returned with streaming eyes and wheezing, like the worst hayfever and asthma. He must have caught a chill here on top of it. His temperature was down to 99 this morning and though it's up to 102 again now I think he is better. He was very bad one night and the doctor said he would like another opinion and brought another old idiot along, who appeared to be a King of the '99s' and kept mislaying his stethoscope. But the nettle rash is abating a little, and he's had an hour or two of sleep today, so I feel much relieved about him.

I hear from Bates in Toronto that Belcher's kidney crocked up again and he was rolling about the floor in agony. My neuritis was killed dead by those sulphur baths at Banff. I've never had a twinge of it left. The fact remains that Bates is the Health Champion of the Mission – having looked like death ever since leaving Southampton!

There has not been very much news to tell you. From Calgary we went to Edmonton and from there to Regina and

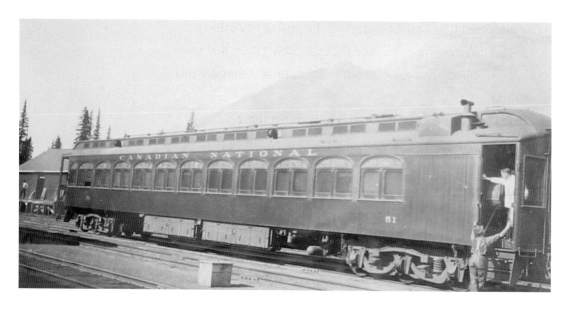

Our private car.

from there to Winnipeg. We stayed a day in each place and usually sleeping in our faithful private car, with Henry, most delightful and attentive of Irish stewards to wait on our every need. All the towns are much the same, set in the middle of flat endless prairies, the 'bald headed Prairie' indeed, interesting to those interested in wheat, but not otherwise. I had a very delightful girl, Miss Rowley, to look after me in Winnipeg, 22 and most lively and good looking, a refreshing change after the worthy wives I have had! We went to the movies and ate rich food together. Belcher had an attack of 'wild man' in Winnipeg, the Governor General having arrived the same day and consequently he was 'overbooked'. He refused to go anywhere the last day and sat in his room dictating to Bates an article to the *Daily Telegraph* on 'Winnipeg the Yankee City', having sat next (at the one dinner he did go to) to a gentleman who informed him that Canada's best hope was to coalesce with the USA, to which B. made the quite able retort that 4 million people do not coalesce with 100 million – they are just absorbed.

The Canadian Government has been most most unsympathetic, in fact it's quite likely they'll refuse to participate at all. The state governments are keen, however, so they may come round. B. is returning here for their decision on Sunday next.

The people in Ottawa are charming. Dr Charles Harriss (who conducts big choirs) took us to the Opera and arranged dinner etc. for the Mission – the kindest of men, but rather like your friend Mr Harding, of 'one of the time' lace capes fame. Then the Admiral, Sir Charles Kingsmill and his wife are delightful. We dined with them, and the Admiral took me driving to see some special maples. He is a dear, like all sailors, knew Login very well and your friend Captain Rose – was his Flag Lieut. out in China, and he and another youth were laughing and ragging together one night when Captain Rose stuck his head out of his cabin and began to curse them for making so much noise, wherupon the Admiral was aroused and, hearing only Rose, stuck *his* head out and reproved him in even more nautical terms while the two lads faded away mirthfully.

I've had charming letters from Mrs Mitchell, and still hope to see her. I should have been in Toronto yesterday, Niagara tomorrow and with Aunt Cassie in New York the end of next week. Now, of course, it depends on A.'s recovery. I'm terrified

'Lady Golfers at ease' at Ottowa Golf Club. Agatha can be seen taking a swing (opposite top left).

of him getting pneumonia. It's been snowing all day today and yesterday the wind was cruel.

We are both sick of the Mission and longing to get home. And the longer the Government dilly dally here, the longer it makes it, with Newfoundland and Nova Scotia still to do. Belcher had taken passages for all of us on Majestic 25th November, but I doubt if they'll do it in time. I shall, anyway – and possibly sooner. I do so want to get *home*. You, my Rosalind, Madge, Monty.

Your loving

Agatha

Doctor been. Says A. decidedly better.

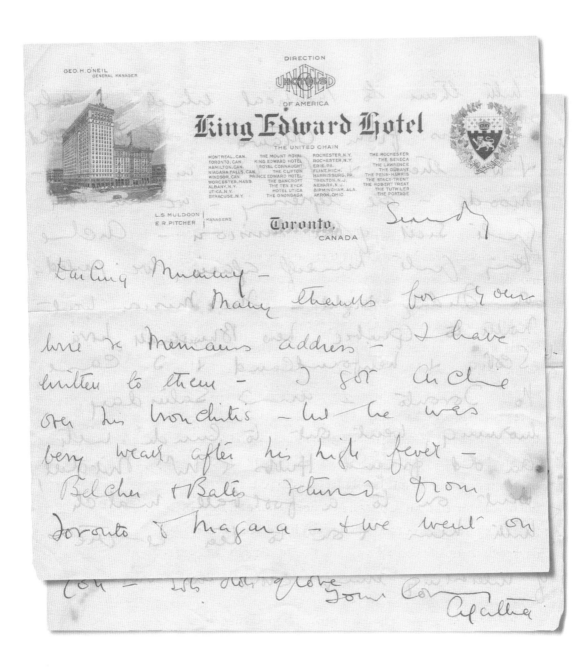

Darling Mummy —

Many thanks for your brief & Memmans address — I have written to them — & for Archie over his bronchitis — but he was very weak after his high fever —

Belcher & Bates returned from Toronto & Niagara — & we went on

... lots of love
Your loving
Agatha

Sunday [November]

Darling Mummy

Many thanks for your line re Memam's address. I have written to them. I got Archie over his bronchitis, but he was very weak after his high fever.

Belcher and Bates returned from Toronto and Niagara and we went on with them to Montreal which is only 3 hours from Ottawa. It was cold and wet there and B. was in his worst moods, all depressing. We are both quite sick of the Mission. Archie being quite himself again, we parted on Friday night. The Mission went north to Quebec, New Brunswick, Nova Scotia and Newfoundland, and I came to Toronto. Arrived Saturday morning, went out to lunch with an old friend Hubbs and Mrs Mitchell, went on to a football match with him and on to tea at the Mitchells. Today I went to church with them, back to lunch. General Mitchell took me round the University and the Museum, and then back to supper. They were so delighted to see me and sent quantities of messages to you. They're full of love for Torquay. General Mitchell told me all sorts of interesting things about the war. I really had a delightful two days with them. Tomorrow morning I go to Niagara (where my free ticket runs out!) and on in the evening to New York to stay with Aunt Cassie.

Belcher has definitely booked births on the Majestic for

Mr W.K. Rodgers with a tame fox.

November 25th. However, it is quite on the cards that he will be delayed in Newfoundland or something and will cancel it all again. But I shall come by it anyway. Home on November 30th! It will be *lovely* to see you.

Lots and lots of love

Your loving

Agatha

LEFT: *Niagara Falls.*
OVERLEAF: *'British Empire Exhibition Boosts Visitors Here'* – Daily News, *November 23rd 1922.*

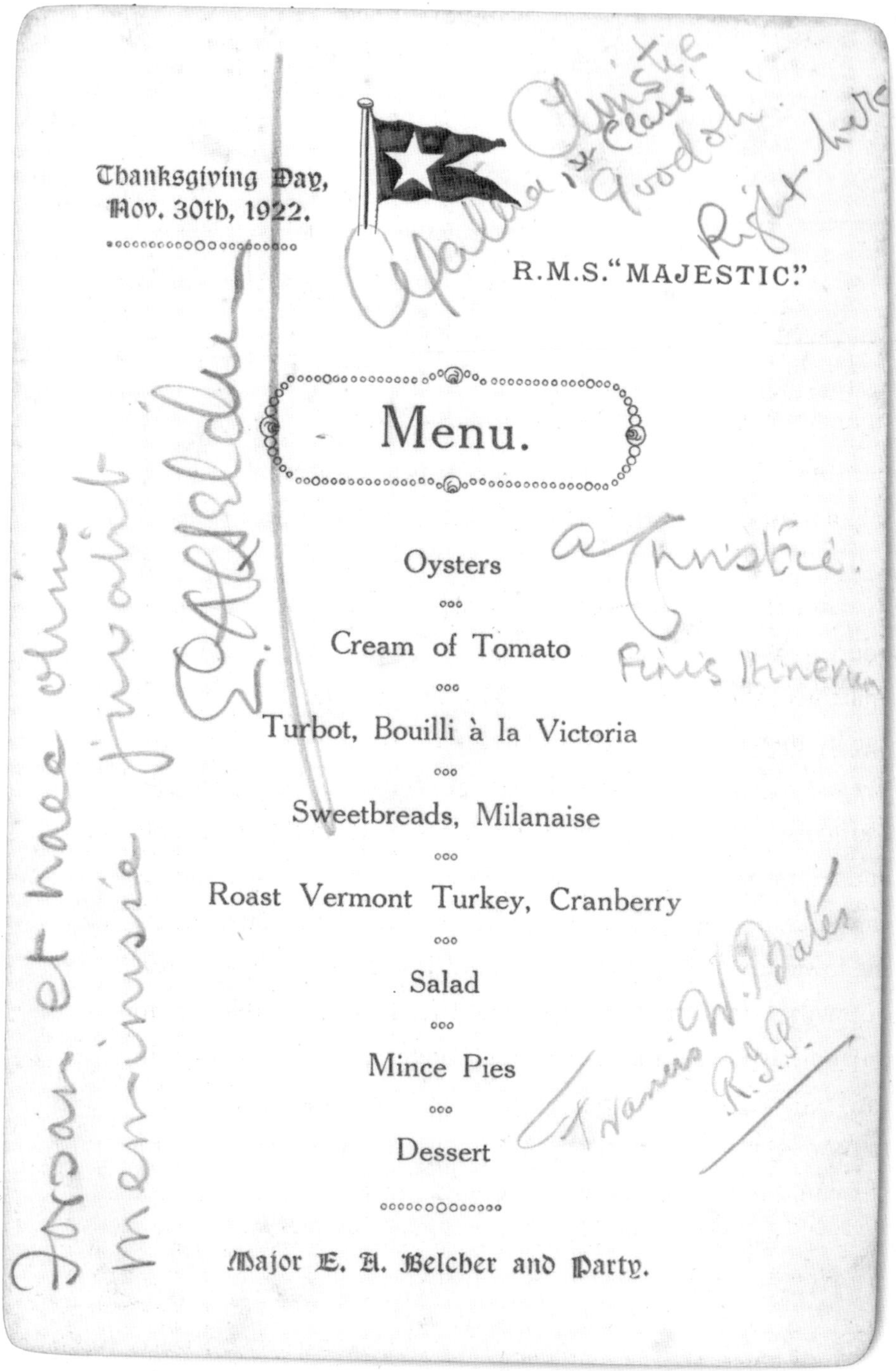

Thanksgiving Day,
Nov. 30th, 1922.

R.M.S. "MAJESTIC"

Agatha Christie
1st Class Goodah
Right here

Menu.

Oysters

Cream of Tomato

Turbot, Bouilli à la Victoria

Sweetbreads, Milanaise

Roast Vermont Turkey, Cranberry

Salad

Mince Pies

Dessert

Major E. A. Belcher and Party.

A Christie.
Finis Itinerum

Francis W. Bates
R.I.P.

THE JOURNEY HOME

So there we were, Archie and I, at Montreal. Our roads were to part: Archie to go with Belcher and inspect silver fox farms, I to take a train south to New York. My money had by now completely run out.

I was met by darling Aunt Cassie at New York. She was so good to me, sweet and affectionate. I stayed with her in the apartment she had in Riverside Drive. She must have been a good age by then – nearly eighty, I should think. She took me to see her sister-in-law, Mrs Pierpont Morgan, and some of the younger Morgans of the family. She also took me to splendid restaurants and fed me delicious food. She talked much of my father and his early days in New York. I had a happy time. Aunt Cassie asked me towards the end of the stay what I would like to do as a treat on my last day. I told her that what I really longed to do was to go and have a meal in a cafeteria. Cafeterias were unknown in England, but I had read about them in New York, and I longed to try one. Aunt Cassie thought this a most extraordinary desire. She could not imagine *anybody* wanting to go to a cafeteria, but since she was full of willingness to please she went there with me.

It was, she said, the first time she had been to one herself. I got my tray and collected things from the counter, and found it all a most amusing new experience.

Then the day came when Archie and Belcher were to reappear in New York. I was glad they were coming, because in spite of all Aunt Cassie's kindness, I was beginning to feel like a bird in a golden cage. Aunt Cassie never dreamed of allowing me to go out by myself anywhere. This was so extraordinary to me, after moving about freely in London, that it made me feel restless.

'But why, Aunt Cassie?'

'Oh, you never know what might happen to someone young and pretty like you are, who doesn't know New York.'

I assured her I was quite all right, but she insisted on either sending me in the car with a chauffeur or taking me herself. I felt inclined sometimes to play truant for three or four hours, but I knew that that would have worried her, so I restrained myself. I began to look forward, though, to being soon in London and able to walk out of my front door any moment I pleased.

Archie and Belcher spent one night in New York, and the next day [November 25th] we embarked on the ~~Berengaria~~ [*Majestic*] for our voyage back to England. I can't say I liked being on the sea again, but I was only moderately sea-sick this time. The rough weather happened at rather a bad moment, however, because we had entered a bridge tournament, and Belcher insisted that I should partner him. I didn't want to, for although Belcher was a good bridge player he disliked losing so much that he always became extremely sulky. However, I was going to be free of him soon, so he and I started on our tournament. Unexpectedly we

ABSTRACT OF LOG.

Quadruple-Screw S.S. "MAJESTIC."

COMMANDER : SIR BERTRAM HAYES, K.C.M.G., D.S.O., R.D.

(Commodore R.N.R. Retd. and Commodore of the White Star Line Fleet).

VOYAGE No. 9 EAST.

New York to Southampton via Cherbourg.

Took Departure from Ambrose Channel Light Vessel 0.57 p.m., November 25th, 1922.

DATE	LAT.	LONG.	MILES	REMARKS
Nov. 26	41˙21	61˙50	554	Strong Westerly to light Variable winds
,, 27	43˙14	49˙27	564	Light Northerly to mod. Southerly winds
,, 28	47˙04	37˙05	572	Strong N.W'ly wind to moderate W'ly gale
,, 29	49˙20	23˙17	568	Strong Westerly to gentle S'ly winds, confused swell
,, 30	49˙42	8˙51	562	Moderate S'ly and S.S.W winds
To Cherbourg Breakwater			284	Arrived at 12.10 a.m. (G.M.T.) Dec. 1st.
Total Distance —			3104	

OCEAN PASSAGE · 5 days · 6 hours · 13 mins.   **AVERAGE SPEED · 24˙59 knots.**

arrived at the final. That was the day that the wind freshened and the boat began to pitch. I did not dare to think of scratching, and only hoped that I would not disgrace myself at the bridge table. Hands were dealt as we started on what might well be the last hand, and almost at once Belcher, with a terrible scowl, slammed his cards down on the table.

'No use my playing this game really,' he said. 'No use at all.' He was scowling furiously, and I think for two pins would have thrown in the hand and allowed the game as a walkover

The journey home.

The S.S. Majestic

to our opponents. However, I myself appeared to have picked up every ace and king in the pack. I played atrociously, but fortunately the cards played themselves. I couldn't lose. In the qualms of sea-sickness I pulled out the wrong card, forgot what trumps were, did everything foolish possible – but my hand was too good. We were triumphant winners of the tournament. I then retired to my cabin, to groan miserably until we docked in England.

The *Majestic* arrived in Southampton on 1st December. Archie told the *Times*: 'The tour has been a great success. We were received enthusiastically everywhere, and are completely satisfied with the result of our work. We have had a strenuous time and are glad to reach home again, but it was worth it.'

OPPOSITE: *The Majestic's First Class lounge and swimming bath.*

I add, as a postscript to the year's adventures, that we did not keep to our vow of never speaking to Belcher again. I am sure everyone who reads this will understand. The furies that take hold of one when cooped up with somebody evaporate when the time of stress is over. To our enormous surprise we found that we actually *liked* Belcher, that we enjoyed his company. On many occasions he dined with us and we with him. We reminisced together in perfect amity over the various happenings of the world tour, saying occasionally to him: 'You really did behave atrociously, you know.'

'I daresay, I daresay,' said Belcher. 'I'm like that, you know.' He waved a hand. 'And anyway I had a lot to try me. Oh, not you two. You didn't worry me much – except Archie being such an idiot as to make himself ill. Absolutely lost I was, that fortnight when I had to do without him. Can't you have something done to your nose and your sinus? What's the good of going through life with a sinus like that? I wouldn't.'

Belcher had come back from his tour, most unexpectedly engaged to be married. A pretty girl, daughter of one of the officials in Australia, had worked with him as his secretary. Belcher was fifty at least, and she, I should say, was eighteen or nineteen. At any rate he announced to us quite suddenly, 'I've a piece of news for you. I'm getting married to Gladys!' And get married to Gladys he did. She arrived by ship shortly after our return. Strangely enough I think it was quite a happy marriage, at least for some years. Gladys was good-tempered, enjoyed living in England, and managed the cantankerous Belcher remarkably well. It must have been, I think, eight or ten years later when we heard the news that a divorce was in progress.

'She's found another chap she liked the look of,' Belcher announced. 'Can't say I blame her, really. She's very young, and of course I am rather an elderly curmudgeon for her. We've remained good friends, and I'm fixing up a nice little sum for her. She's a good girl.'

I remarked to Belcher on one of the first occasions we dined together after our return: 'Do you know you still owe me two pounds eighteen and fivepence for white socks?'

'Dear, dear,' he said. 'Do I really? Are you expecting to get it?'

'No,' I said.

'Quite right,' said Belcher. 'You won't.' And we both laughed.

BRITISH EMPIRE EXHIBITION 1924

OFFICIAL GUIDE

EPILOGUE

by Mathew Prichard

So they were home in time for Christmas: my grandparents, exhausted and desperate to see their daughter Rosalind, followed by Belcher, no doubt in triumphant mood. But was it worth it? Did it make a difference? What was the 1924 British Empire Exhibition itself like?

Well, after 90 years probably nobody can accurately assess what difference this comparatively minor marketing expedition made to the overall success or failure of the Exhibition. It visited very few of the 58 countries in the Empire, and construction on the site had begun the same month the tour started, so plans were already well underway regardless. However, it is worthwhile recording a few facts...

The Exhibition was opened on St George's Day, 23 April 1924, by King George V and Queen Mary at the Empire Stadium, Wembley. It covered more than 216 acres, and its four main objectives were to produce new sources of wealth by exploiting the raw materials of the Empire; to foster inter-Imperial trade; to

Col. C.G. Liddell, C.M.G. C.B.E. DSO.
Deputy Administrator.

Major Frank Fox
General Secretary Fellowship of the
B.E.E & Assistant to Chief.
Administrator

Lt. Col. W.C. Bersey
Controller of Administrative
Services

Lt Col. C.C. Mason, D.S.O
Legal Adviser.

A.G. Chuter Esq.
Finance Manager

Sir Lawrence Weaver, K.B.E.
Director United Kingdom Exhibits.

Col. L.G. Tempest Stone, C.M.G
M. Inst T
Transport Superintendent

Major E.A. Belcher, C.B.E.
Controller of General Services

OFFICIAL GUIDE.

INTRODUCTION.

IN the old days, the Grand Tour was the prize of the fortunate few. Young men of wealth and position devoted two or three years to travel, often in circumstances of acute discomfort, and came back having caught no more than a glimpse of Europe. The Empire as we know it did not exist. Even the beginnings were small and far away. To-day the Grand Tour is within the reach of all, and the actual cost of it is just eighteenpence !

In all probability not one in a hundred of those who come to Wembley has grasped the extent of Great Britain's achievement or felt the resultant pride of citizenship, and it is safe to say that all, without exception, will be astonished to find how adequately within the bounds of a single park, large though it be, it has been found possible to present Empires, Dominions, Colonies, Dependencies and Protectorates, each in its habit as it thrives to-day.

Of course, all the world of Wembley is in Gala dress. The visitor sees here the ripe product of British achievement in all parts of the earth. The work that underlies the fine finish of an exhibit, say, from Australia or Canada or even farther afield, may be the result of generations of striving, but of this striving we see little, except where deliberately it is set out for us to see.

The fundamental purpose of the British Empire Exhibition is serious. It is to stimulate trade, to strengthen the bonds that bind the Mother Country to her Sister States and Daughter Nations, to bring all into closer touch the one with the other, to enable all who owe allegiance to the British flag to meet on common ground, and to learn to know each other. It is a Family Party, to which every part of the Empire is invited, and at which every part of the Empire is represented.

It is well to insist that here we have no ephemeral structure designed to endure for a season and to pass thereafter into desolation or decay. The material chiefly used at Wembley for purposes of construction is concrete with steel. No lesser foundation would serve the purpose of Empire. The whole layout has demanded and received the closest study over a long period of time by the architects, Sir John W. Simpson, K.B.E., and Mr. Maxwell Ayrton, and the engineer, Sir E. Owen Williams, K.B.E., to whose genius the Home Country's buildings stand as a permanent memorial.

open new world markets for Dominican and British products; and to encourage interaction between the different cultures and people of the Empire by juxtaposing Britain's industrial prowess with the diverse products of the Dominicans and Colonies.

The Exhibition was open for six months in 1924 and reopened in May 1925, presumably in response to popular demand. It was reported that over 20 million people visited the Exhibition, that it cost £2,200,000 to put on (half of which was guaranteed by the Government), and that by the time it closed in October 1925 it had lost £1,500,000. The real figures are believed to be much higher. Admission for adults was one and a half shillings, with children half price. Amongst 15 senior administrative staff who were responsible for the Exhibition, the Controller of General Services was none other than Major E. A. Belcher, CBE!

I never met my grandfather, Archie Christie, but from anecdotal evidence garnered from friends and colleagues of his in the City of London much later in his life, I gather that he built a considerable reputation for himself as a shrewd man of business. As this book has shown, on his return Archie was quoted as saying, 'The tour has been a great success.' I am therefore inclined to accept him at his word and believe that it was indeed a great success – for the participants of the Grand Tour, for the British Empire Exhibition itself, and thanks to my grandmother's painstaking letters and admirable photography, for those of us who are able to read about it now.

MATHEW PRICHARD

CHRONOLOGY

This chronology has been compiled as a summary of they key places and events discussed in the letters. Some of the dates are tentative. Where necessary, dates and other information have been drawn from contemporary newpaper reports; these are marked with an asterisk.

Agatha Christie's family

Agatha Christie, author of a novel, *The Mysterious Affair at Styles* (1920).

Lieutenant-Colonel Archibald ('Archie') Christie, Agatha's first husband, financial adviser to the Overseas Mission of the British Empire Exhibition.

Rosalind ('Teddy'), their daughter.

'Punkie', Agatha's elder sister Madge Miller.

Monty, Agatha's brother Louis Montant Miller.

Members of the British Empire Exhibition Mission party

Major Ernest Albert Belcher, CBE, assistant general manager (nicknamed 'the Wild Man').

Mr F.W. Bates, Belcher's secretary.

Frederick Hiam (knighted 1924), agricultural adviser, and his wife Charlotte.

Sylvia Hiam, their daughter.

Chronology

Friday 20 January 1922. The Mission party leaves Waterloo and sails on the *RMS Kildonan Castle* from **Southampton**. Fellow passengers: Ashby, the naval attaché; Miss Wright; Miss Gold; Samels; Mrs Blake, wife of the captain of the *Queen Elizabeth*; the Fichardts, a Dutch couple, and their many children; Mr Edge, a rich elderly bachelor; Mr Murray, the commissioner; the Chief Engineer.

Late January. Agatha suffers sea sickness in the Bay of Biscay and stays on board when the ship docks at **Madeira**.

Saturday 4 February. They have crossed the Equator.

Monday 6 February. Arrival in **Cape Town** in the evening, greeted by Major Featherston, the Deputy Trade Commissioner.

Tuesday 7 February. Agatha and Archie have been surfing at nearby Muizenberg. Car tour with Belcher, Ashby and British manufacturers' representatives to Hout's Bay, Constantia, Kalk Bay, and Wynberg.

Wednesday 8 February (?) By car with Belcher and Archie to Groote Scuur, Sir Cecil Rhodes's house, and to the Rhodes Memorial.

Thursday 9 February. Agatha surfs with Ashby and Sylvia Hiam in Muizenberg. To Cape Town town hall to meet the Mayor and Mrs Gardiner, followed by a concert. Friction between Belcher and Featherston ('Wetherslab').

Saturday 11 February. Shopping with Sylvia Hiam. Bathing with Archie at Fish Hoek.

Sunday 12 February. With Belcher and Sylvia Hiam to Simonstown to meet Admiral Sir William Goodenough, commander-in-chief of the Africa Station, and his wife.

Wednesday 15 February. Half-holiday. Archie surfs at Muizenberg. Hiam and Bates claim to have almost conquered Table Mountain. In the afternoon Agatha visits Cape Town's museum with Mrs Blake and her cousins Marye Cole and Mrs Thomas.

Thursday 16 February. Tour of fruit farms including the Mallasons' at Ida's Valley and the Rhodes Fruit Farm. The Hiams are exhausted.

Friday 17 February. Opening of parliament; Agatha sits with Mrs and

Sylvia Hiam in the front row. Prince Arthur of Connaught speaks as Governor-General of South Africa; his wife Princess Arthur watches. Agatha and Archie buy surfboards in Muizenberg.

Saturday 18 February. The Archbishop's garden party at Bishop's Court; Princess Arthur of Connaught and Admiral Goodenough attend. With Archie, Belcher, Marye Cole and flag lieutenant Nigel Battine for dinner and to a dance in Wynberg; Lord Mandeville, the Duke of Manchester's son, is there.

Sunday 19 February. A walk up Table Mountain; Agatha retires early, followed by Bates, but Archie reaches the top.

Monday 20 February. Lunch at Admiral Goodenough's with Colonel and Lady Dorothy Meynell. Bridge in the evening with Dr Gordon (Belcher's doctor) and his mother.

Tuesday 21 February. The Mission members have lunch at Government House with Prince and Princess Arthur of Connaught; their lady-in-waiting Lady Evelyn Farquhar; F.S. Malan, South African Minister of Mines; Henry Burton, Finance Minister; Sir Thomas and Lady Smartt; and J. W. Jagger, Minister of Railways. Later by car with Dr Vander Byl to an explosives factory in the mountains.

Thursday 23 February. Crisis over itinerary as Rhodesia offers insufficient tickets for the Mission; furious telegrams from Belcher.

Friday 24 February. First letter after several hot, uneventful days with regular trips to an open-air sea swimming bath at Sea Point.

Saturday 25 February. To the Kenilworth races with Archie and Bates. Admiral Goodenough and Prince Arthur are there.

Sunday 26 February. Muizenberg for lunch with Sir Abe Bailey, followed by surfing with Mrs Blake.

Monday 27 February. Rhodesia has capitulated to Belcher's demands, and the original itinerary is restored.

Tuesday 28 February. Archie leaves Cape Town for Durban on the R.M.S. *Briton* with Mrs and Sylvia Hiam.

Wednesday 1 March. Agatha, Belcher and Mr Hiam take the train for Pretoria.

Thursday 2 March. Across the semi-desert Karroo plateau.

Friday 3 March. **Bloemfontein** – tour of a creamery and Major Quinn's government farm. General J.B.M. Hertzog, the South African opposition leader, refuses to meet Belcher.

Saturday 4 March. To **Harrismith**, where they sleep on the train.

Sunday 5 March. Breakfast in Harrismith. Motor tour of veldt farms.

Monday 6 March. Overnight train from Harrismith.

Tuesday 7 March. They arrive in **Durban** at 7.15am; reunion with Archie. Mr Mayne, an American friend, takes them by car to gardens of blue monkeys. Agatha and Archie take the 5.50pm train for Johannesburg.

Wednesday 8 March. Arrive in **Johannesburg** at 5pm in the midst of a violent strike. Trade commissioner Major Langton has them driven under armed protection to the Grand Hotel in **Pretoria** for safety. Martial law declared.

Thursday 9 to Monday 13 March. Strike becomes an uprising – the Rand Revolt. Railways and roads are impassable so they remain in Pretoria, now a city under heavy guard. *Kildonan Castle* passenger Miss Wright, a university teacher there, keeps the Christies company. Mrs Harvey, wife of their host, shows them the Union Buildings (seat of the South African government); the Under-Secretary for the Interior, Mr Venn, shows them the archives. Mr Blundell, Under-Secretary for Industries, drives them to a country club for tea.

Tuesday 14 March. Permits suddenly arrive for them to leave. Car to **Johannesburg**. They leave by train while battle is fought in nearby Fordsburg, the rebel headquarters. Arrive in **Bloemfontein** late.

Wednesday 15 March. By train to **Kimberley**.

Thursday 16 March. Visit to a De Beers mine, closed by the strike action. Night train from Kimberley.

Friday 17 March. Through **Bechuanaland** (Botswana) with fellow passengers the Thompsons.

Saturday 18 March. Customs check at 3am as train enters Southern Rhodesia (Zimbabwe). Overnight train arrives in **Bulawayo**. Car trip to the Matopo (Matobo) Hills and Sir Cecil Rhodes' grave. They catch the night train.

Sunday 19 March. They arrive in Rhodesian capital **Salisbury** (Harare) after a day's travel. Miss Montagu, sister of the Meikle's Hotel acting administrator, shows Agatha the town and Lady Chaplin's menagerie at Government House. Tea with Miss Montagu and the wife of attorney-general James Donald Mackenzie. Lunch at the Montagus' with hotel administrator Mr Hone, then by car to visit the wife of resident commissioner Douglas Jones and a plot of Montagu land.

Tuesday 21 March. Mazoe Valley Citrus Estate, and tea with manager Mr Swain and his family. Bridge with tobacco factor Mr Taylor and his wife.

Thursday 23 March. Arrival in **Bulawayo**, then another overnight train.

Friday 24 March. To **Victoria Falls**.

Saturday 25 March. By 'trolley' to the Zambezi (comedian George Graves is in hospital after losing a finger when a similar trolley derailed). Then by steam launch to **Livingstone**, capital of Northern Rhodesia (now Maramba, Zambia), where they meet the Thompsons again. Lunch on Kandahar Island and tea on another, then back to Victoria Falls Hotel.

Monday 27 March. They leave Victoria Falls after Belcher telegraphs recalling them to Cape Town; he has left for Australia.

Tuesday 28 March to Saturday 1 April. Journey back to Cape Town, including **Bulawayo** and two days at **Johannesburg**, where Agatha is barred from going with Archie down the Crown Mine. A fellow passenger, ex-naval Captain Crowther (who works for a paper firm in Africa owned by Agatha's friend Wilfred Pirie) will take their souvenirs home to England.

Sunday 2 April. Agatha and Archie reach **Cape Town** and the Mount Nelson Hotel in the evening. The Hiams have returned to England. Agatha is confident her second novel, *The Secret Adversary*, introducing detectives 'Tommy and Tuppence', will be a success.

Monday 3 April. Positive press reviews of *The Secret Adversary* have arrived.

Saturday 8 April. Agatha and Archie leave Cape Town on the *Aeneas*, bound for Australia. Agatha is sea-sick for the first half of the voyage but revels in the remainder in the company of the dancing Captain;

Mr Stourton, a polo pony buyer; Mrs Longworth, wife of Australia's swimming champion, and their young son; and Miss King, a nurse.

Saturday 29 April. The *Aeneas* docks in **Adelaide** in the morning; Belcher has gone ahead so Agatha and Archie leave by train that afternoon.

Sunday 30 April. They reach **Melbourne** and the Menzies Hotel. Belcher in bed with a bad leg.

Monday 1 May. To Parliament House to watch Labour Day processions and drink ginger ale with Thomas Givens, the President of the Australian Senate. Afternoon motor tour with Customs official Mr Greenwood and his daughters: to the Showgrounds to watch Labour Day sport with secretary Jack Smith (Agatha photographs champion runner Ruby Baddock); then around the bay.

Tuesday 2 May. They embark with Belcher for Tasmania in the afternoon.

Wednesday 3 May. They reach **Launceston** in the morning and take the train via **Parattah**, arriving in **Hobart** that evening. Premier's secretary Mr Addison greets them. Belcher feels snubbed by Tasmanian entrepreneur Sir Henry Jones. Agatha and Archie stroll around town.

Friday 5 May. By car to see hydro-electric power station at Waddamana with its manager John Butters, Commonwealth emigration officer Colonel Hurley, and librarian J. Moore Robinson. Late back to Hobart; Archie takes night train for a weekend in Launceston.

Saturday 6 May. Mr Moore Robinson shows Agatha the Tasmanian Museum. Afternoon at the races with Belcher, Tasmania's Treasurer (and former Premier) Sir Elliott Lewis, and Mrs Lyon, wife of the Racing Club president. Bridge at the Ladies Lyceum Club with mayoress Mrs Snowden and a Mrs Mulock.

Sunday 7 May. Agatha and Bates return to **Launceston** by car.

Monday 8 May. A walk up the Cataract Gorge. Agatha leaves Tasmania on the S.S. *Nairana* with Archie and Bates.

Tuesday 9 May. **Melbourne** again. Macpherson Robertson shows them round his chocolate factory (MacRobertson's).

Wednesday 10 May. Belcher arrives from Tasmania.

Thursday 11 May. Lunch with journalist Freda Sternberg, who is writing about Agatha and *The Secret Adversary* for the *Melbourne Herald*.

Friday 12 May. Agatha is photographed for the *Herald* and has tea with Freda.

Sunday 14 May. With Freda Sternberg to visit ex-journalist Mrs Walker and family at Wombalano.

Monday 15 May. Sunshine Harvester Works visit.

Thursday 18 May. By train with Belcher and Victoria state premier Harry Lawson to Castlemaine to see an engineering works run by a Mr Thompson, as well as a woollen factory and a pottery. Theatre in Melbourne in the evening.

Friday 19 May. By car to Warburton wood distilleries, timber forests and mills, with directors Wilfrid Russell Grimwade and Mr Stewart, Stirling Taylor and trade commissioner MacGregor. Dinner at Government House, Melbourne, with Archbishop Harrington Lees and his wife; Governor of Victoria the Earl of Stradbroke, his wife the Countess, and his secretary Mr Grove; and a Mr Winter-Irving.

Saturday 20 May. Agatha and Archie by car with a Mr James, his lady friend, a cinematographer and chauffeur Arthur to the Gippsland region. They inspect brickworks and other industries at Dandenong; have lunch in Warrigal; and take the Noojee 'bush tram' to the Goodwood Sawmills. Overnight at a **Noojee** boarding house.

Sunday 21 May. Up another Gippsland valley by bush tram.

Monday 22 May. Train via Seymour to **Shepperton**. Hotel lunch with dignitaries. A canned fruit factory and a freezing works. A Miss Sutherland and her sister look after Agatha.

Tuesday 23 May. Visit to fruit farms on the Returned Soldiers' Irrigation Settlement; lunch at Dookie Agricultural College with pioneering wheat breeder Hugh Pye; then back by train via Seymour to **Melbourne**.

Wednesday 24 May. Lunch at the Royal Colonial Institute at the Grand Hotel with Lord Stradbroke; speech by celebrated surgeon Sir James Barrett.

Thursday 25 May. The Mission leaves Melbourne, under the care of a Mr Cocks, and stays overnight in **Echuca** on the New South Wales border.

Friday 26 May. Visit to a new lock on the Murray River; lunch with the mayors of Echuca and Moama; by car to see Merino rams at **Cobram Station**, where they stay overnight.

Saturday 27 May. To **Yanga Station** with its manager, Mr Bezley, and land agent Hector Mackenzie.

Sunday 28 May. A day off, with a morning drive around the lake at Yanga.

Monday 29 May. To a 'Cultivation camp' in the morning; then by car to Hay, arriving late at night after breakdowns and false turns.

Tuesday 30 May (?) They spend the night at a government 'hydro'.

Wednesday 31 May. The Mission arrives in **Sydney** in the morning and leaves that evening on the northbound train.

Thursday 1 June. Night train.

Friday 2 June. The Mission members switch trains at breakfast at Wallangarra on the Queensland border, greeted by Mr Troedson of the tourist bureau. After halts for civic receptions at Stanthorpe, Warwick and Toowoomba, they arrive in **Brisbane** at 10pm, staying at the Belle Vue Hotel.*

Saturday 3 June. * Agatha explores Brisbane in the morning. In the afternoon she, the Mission and Queensland Ministers take a McKeen motorised railcar to the Beerburrum Soldier Settlement. Dinner in Brisbane with Mr Troedson, a General and Mrs Spencer Brown.

Sunday 4 June. * By car to Mount Coot overlooking Brisbane. Lunch at the Pier Hotel, Cleveland, with Mr Troedson and MPs Mr Kurwan and Mr Barnes, followed by fruit farm visit. Sunday tea at the Belle Vue.

Monday 5 June. * While the rest of the Mission goes on an official visit to Ipswich, Agatha goes to the races with Mrs Theodore, the Premier's wife. She meets Major Bell and his sister Una, who invite her to stay at Coochin.

Tuesday 6 June. Agatha and the Mission attend a vice-regal garden party at Government House, Brisbane. Agatha takes the evening train with Una Bell to **Coochin Coochin Station**, where she stays for a week with Mrs Eva Bell, her daughters Una, Enid ('Doll'), Aileen, her two younger sons Victor and Bert, majors in the Flying Corps. Two older sons, Frick and Ernest, live nearby with their families. Also visiting are Margaret Allen and her cousin Dundas Allen, from Sydney, and Mr Foa, an Englishman. An elderly Aboriginal woman, Susan, makes an impression on Agatha.

Wednesday 7 June. Archie leaves Brisbane with Bates for several days' tour of Rockhampton, Maryborough and elsewhere.*

Sunday 11 June. Belcher arrives at Coochin.

Tuesday 13 June. Belcher and Agatha leave Coochin Coochin Station for **Brisbane**, where she catches the evening train south with the rest of the Mission.*[1]

Thursday 15 June. The Mission returns to **Sydney**.*

Friday 16 June. Archie and Belcher join the Premier at a dinner for Indian statesman and orator Srinivasa Sastri.*

Sunday 18 or Monday 19 June (?) By car to the Blue Mountains to see the Jenolan Caves, staying overnight at the Caves House Hotel.

Sunday 25 June. Agatha has supper with the Allens (the Bells' former guests) and a Mrs Dangar.

Thursday 29 June. The Mission sails from Sydney for New Zealand on the *Manuka*[2]. Fellow passengers include 'the Dehydrator'.

*Monday 3 July.** The *Manuka* arrives in **Wellington**; trade commissioner Mr Dalton greets the Mission.

Tuesday 4 July. Agatha is shown Wellington and its botanical gardens by a Mrs Collins; then to Parliament House.

Wednesday 5 July. Golf with Mrs Collins and Bridge with Mrs Dalton while the Mission dines with the Governor-General, Viscount Jellicoe. They take the night cargo steamer across Cook's Strait, accompanied by a Mr O'Brien as guide.

---

[1] Agatha's autobiography seems to err in recalling that Archie came to Coochin Coochin Station; newspaper reports show him fully occupied elsewhere.

[2] The autobiography misplaces the Tasmania visit between Sydney and New Zealand, several weeks late.

Thursday 6 July. The Mission arrives in **Nelson** on the South Island in the morning and visits a woollen factory in the afternoon. They stay at the Commercial Hotel.

Friday 7 July. They visit the Cawthron Institute and are shown experiments by Professor Thomas Easterfield, Dr Robert Tillyard, and Dr Kathleen Curtis. Lunch with the Chamber of Commerce.

Saturday 8 July. By omnibus car over the Dovedale hills to Motueka, where a Mr Isaac Monnoy shows them nuggets.

Sunday 9 July. Agatha lunches with Captain and Mrs Moncrieff from England, and takes tea with Dr and Mrs Tillyard and their daughters Patience, Faith, Hope and Honor. Belcher and Archie play golf.

Monday 10 July. By car through the Buller Gorge in the rain. Visit to a coal mine with the Westport Progress League. Baths at **Westport**.

Tuesday 11 July. Archie and Agatha visit Denniston, where he inspects another coal mine while she is entertained by the manager's wife.

Wednesday 12 July. By car through the Buller Gorge to Reefton, then by train to **Greymouth**.

Thursday 13 July. Car tour along the coast to **Punakaiki**; tea with a Mrs Olney, then a Mission meeting while Agatha socializes with Mrs Kitchingham, one of three ladies who have accompanied her for the day.

Friday 14 July. By car to **Hokitika**, an old gold mining town, then to Lake Kaniere. Archie is adopted by 'Mother Seigel'.

Saturday 15 July. By car to the Otira Gorge, then an 11-mile walk with Archie and Belcher to Arthur's Pass. Train to **Christchurch**.

Sunday 16 July. Tea with architect Cecil Wood and his wife Iris.

Monday 17 July. Agatha has morning tea with the Women's Club (Archie later sends the newspaper report to her mother). In the afternoon the Mayor, Henry Thacker, takes her to an elderly ladies' institute.

Tuesday 18 July. Archie leaves for Invercargill.

Wednesday 19 to Monday 24 July. Agatha spends a day at **Rotorua**. Then spends some time in **Auckland** with Archie.

Tuesday 25 July to Friday 4 August. Agatha and Archie, beginning a break from Mission duties, sail from Auckland on the *Makura*. Also on board are Srinivasa Sastri and his secretary Bajpai; the Taits of Taveuni in Fiji; Fiona Cacanuti. The Christies befriend Oxford graduates Lord Swinfen and Mr St Aubyn, and Australian sisters Miss Morton and Mrs Minnett. The ship docks for a day at **Suva, Fiji** en route.

Saturday 5 August. At the Moano Hotel, **Honolulu, Hawaii.** Daughter Rosalind's third birthday.

August. Surfing, sunburn, and socialising with Mr St Aubyn, Lord Swinfen, Mrs Minnett, Miss Morton, and the Luckies, a New Zealand couple. They take a trip in a glass-bottomed boat at Haleiwa, they join a country club, and with Mr Luckie they visit a pineapple factory.

Tuesday 29 August. Agatha and Archie, now staying in a cottage or chalet bungalow halfway between Honolulu town and Waikiki, are running low on funds. They have decided to remain in Hawaii until Belcher arrives on the *Niagara*, rather than leaving for San Francisco. Agatha has developed neuritis in her shoulder and arm.

Saturday 9 September.* Belcher having reached Hawaii, Agatha and Archie rejoin the Mission as it leaves on the *Niagara*. Fellow passengers include Broadway actress Elsie Mackay (Mrs Lionel Atwill).

Friday 15 September. Agatha's 32nd birthday.*

Saturday 16 September. The *Niagara* docks at **Victoria, British Columbia, Canada,** where the Mission members stay at the Empress Hotel.

Sunday 17 September. Tea supper in Victoria. Agatha is pleased with her income for *The Mysterious Affair at Styles*, her first novel (1920) and expects *The Secret Adversary* to bring in healthy royalties this month.

Monday 18 September. Car tour of the lumber industry.

Sunday 24 September. To **Banff**, in the Canadian Rockies, staying at the Banff Springs Hotel. During the visit, a treatment in the sulphur baths cures Agatha's sinusitis.

Thursday 28 September to Sunday 1 October. The Mission stops in **Calgary**, staying with Professor W.H. Carlyle at the Prince of Wales's Alberta ranch, with a dinner at the Palliser Hotel on the Friday evening.

Early to mid-October. The Mission travels through Alberta and

Saskatchewan, staying briefly in **Edmonton**, **Regina**, and **Winnipeg**. A young Canadian, Miss Rowley, keeps Agatha company in Winnipeg. After inspecting a grain elevator there, Archie suffers a sinus reaction, which develops into severe bronchitis and nettle rash.

Mid-October. Conductor Dr Charles Harriss takes the Mission members to the opera in **Ottawa**. They dine with Admiral Sir Charles Kingsmill and his wife; the Admiral takes Agatha by car to look at maple trees, and Agatha plays golf.

Thursday 19 October. At Chateau Laurier in Ottawa, Archie is beginning to recover. Belcher and Bates have gone on to Toronto. Agatha has had to delay her own plans. Belcher and Bates return from Toronto and the Mission travels to **Montreal**. Archie, now fully recovered from bronchitis, departs with Belcher and Bates for further Quebec locations and thence to New Brunswick, Nova Scotia, and Newfoundland. To preserve the Christies' dwindling travel funds, Agatha leaves the Mission for Toronto.

Saturday in mid-November. Agatha arrives in **Toronto**, where she stays at the King Edward Hotel. She has lunch with Mrs Mitchell and Hubbs, an old friend, who takes her to a football match. Tea at home of General and Mrs Mitchell.

Sunday in mid-November. Church and lunch with the Mitchells.

Monday in mid-November. Agatha visits **Niagara** and in the evening reaches **New York**, where stays with Aunt Cassie at Riverside Drive. They dine at restaurants and, at Agatha's special request, a cafeteria. They visit Aunt Cassie's sister-in-law Mrs Pierpont Morgan.

Friday 24 November. Archie and Belcher reach New York.

Saturday 25 November. The Mission leaves America on board the *Majestic*.

Friday 1 December. The *Majestic* docks in **Southampton**.

Wednesday 23 April 1924 (St George's Day). The British Empire Exhibition is opened by King George V at Wembley Park, and runs until October, with a second season in May-October 1925.

Chronology compiled by John Garth

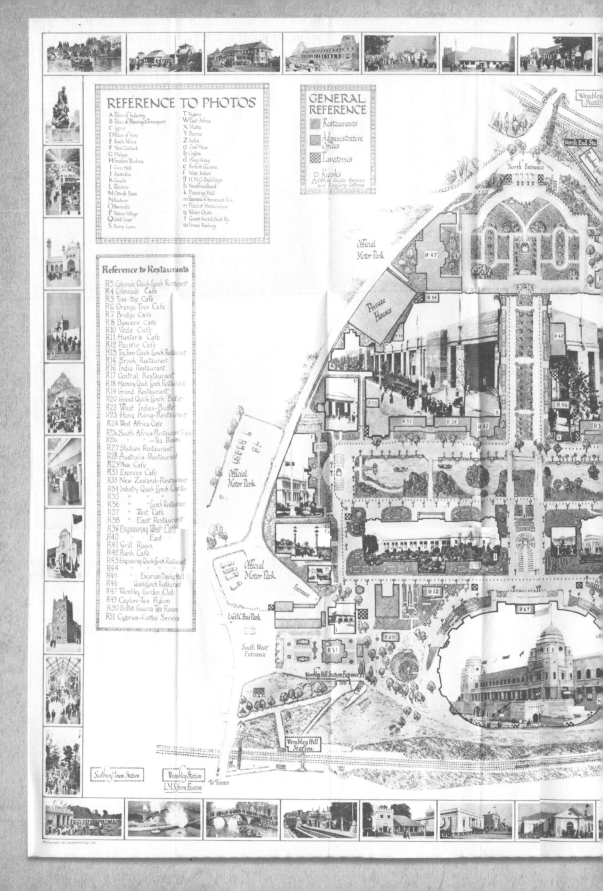